United in
Heart

Divided in
Faith

United in
Heart

Divided in
Faith

*A Guide for
Catholic-Protestant Couples*

SANDRA L. STANKO

SunCreek
B O O K S
Allen, Texas

Acknowledgments

The Scripture quotations contained herein are from the *New Revised Standard Version Bible: Catholic Edition,* copyright © 1993 and 1989 by the Division of Christian Education for the National Council of the Churches of Christ in the U.S.A. Used by permission. All rights reserved.

Send all inquiries to:
SunCreek Books
An RCL Company
200 East Bethany Drive
Allen, Texas 75002-3804

Telephone: 800-264-0368 / 972-390-6300
Fax: 800-688-8356 / 972-390-6560

E-mail: cservice@rcl-enterprises.com

Website: **www.ThomasMore.com**

Printed in the United States of America

Library of Congress Catalog Number: 2002109631

5703   ISBN 1-932057-03-X

1 2 3 4 5   07 06 05 04 03

For Matthew,
who is here because of the principles
learned and conveyed in the pages of this book.

ACKNOWLEDGMENTS

I am indebted to so many people who helped to make this book into a reality. First, I'd like to thank Anthony Ucciardo, my high school English teacher, who recognized raw potential in me all those years ago and was the first to encourage me to pursue my interest in writing. I also want to thank my reviewers, whose incredibly insightful comments helped me to fine-tune and clarify the issues discussed in the book: Pastor Bert Jones, Pastor Bob Stanko, Darin Hepler, Tracie LeShock Bowser, Geraldine Hansotte, and Donald Hansotte. And a big, big kiss of gratitude goes to my husband Brian, who believed in this book from the very start and never wavered in his encouragement. Above all, I want to thank God, for opening doors and blessing me with the opportunity to glorify him in this way. All credit and glory and honor are due you, Lord, at this moment and forevermore.

CONTENTS

INTRODUCTION

To a Christian Couple in Religious Conflict

Relationships are tough, any way you look at them. Each person brings to the relationship different beliefs, perspectives, outlooks, goals, dreams, and expectations. And in a society that emphasizes career development and independence for both men and women, often each person has lived independently and developed strong personal habits and beliefs, which make it even harder for a relationship to work.

But as hard as an average relationship is, it can be even more difficult and complicated when each person is a Christian coming from a different religious background, each strong in his or her faith and set of belief practices; united in heart, but divided in faith.

This is the situation in which I found myself when I met Brian, the man who later became my husband. During our first telephone conversation, when Brian was living in Tampa and I was a thousand miles away in Pittsburgh, we realized that there was something special between us. But we also realized that we had a momentous conflict on our hands when we began discussing religion and Brian said to me, "You're not Catholic, are you?" In fact, I am. And he is Protestant, having attended Presbyterian, Baptist, Methodist, and nondenominational Protestant churches. Because of the prejudices we each carried toward the other person's religion, we didn't know whether our relationship would go anywhere, or die right then.

Our relationship has gone somewhere, blessed and remarkable. We are now married and have a wonderful son, and each of us has grown by tremendous leaps and bounds in our personal faith and understanding of the other's religion. But our journey to this point has been rocky. We've had numerous heated discussions and arguments, saying hurtful things and shedding many tears. But we've clung together and pushed ahead, continuously committing to each other and to God that we will open our hearts and minds to new ways of learning about and worshipping him.

My husband and I might not have received as many bumps and bruises along the way, however, if we had had a resource that could have guided us in understanding and resolving our Catholic-Protestant interfaith issues. While no books were available for us, you now hold such a guide in your hands. *United in Heart, Divided in Faith* is the result of the insights we have gained from our interfaith relationship, bits of advice and information to help you resolve the issues that may be dividing you.

United in Heart, Divided in Faith is intended for couples just beginning their journey together, as well as those in established relationships who are still wrestling with religious issues. Within the book's pages, you will uncover its powerful premise: The religious conflicts that you are experiencing are likely not related to differences in your actual core faith but instead stem from those primarily Catholic religious beliefs, traditions, and practices that are not explicitly defined in Scripture and have been established or interpreted by men other than the apostles. By focusing on core faith rather than on religious traditions and practices, you will both likely discover that your faith is quite similar, and perhaps even identical.

The goals of *United in Heart, Divided in Faith* are to help both of you understand and discuss various aspects of your faith beliefs and religious practices. The book is not intended to promote one religion as "right" and one as "wrong," nor is it to convert either of you to one religion or the other—in fact, in our marriage, my husband has deliberately chosen to remain Protestant, while I have remained Catholic. Rather, it is designed to help you identify the beliefs you have in common, understand your differences, and, most importantly, grow in a unified Christian relationship that glorifies Jesus Christ. "It is not necessary that we all sing the same song," says Sister Charlene Altemose in *Why Do Catholics . . . ?,* "but the music we make ought to blend into a harmony of peace, understanding, and love."[1]

United in Heart, Divided in Faith is divided into three parts. The first part, "Emphasizing the Similarities in Our Faith," outlines the basic beliefs that Catholics and Protestants do have in common. Recognizing and agreeing upon these core Christian faith beliefs is your key to building a solid Christian interfaith relationship.

But although it is important and necessary for you to focus on the similarities in your faith, you must also acknowledge and discuss your differences. The second part, "Addressing the Differences in Our Beliefs," will guide you through this process by clearly explaining some of the topics that have been traditionally debated between Catholics and Protestants, primarily man-interpreted beliefs that are likely at the root of your conflicts.

And if you have worked through the first two parts and truly believe that God is leading you into a marriage partnership, you will find the information in the third part to be relevant in planning your future together. "Discussing Important Issues in Our Interfaith Marriage" anticipates the unique questions an interfaith couple must answer when their relationship leads to marriage.

Along with presenting personal insights and anecdotes, each chapter in this book is solidly rooted in Scripture, contains thoughts from various Catholic and Protestant sources, and ends with "Relationship Builders," chapter highlights and discussion questions intended to help you apply each topic to your interfaith relationship.

As Christians steadfast in your religious beliefs, you may have difficulty accepting some of the information in this book without question. And honestly, I hope that you do question it. Because guidelines for a Christian interfaith relationship do not specifically appear in the Bible, you need to take the information that I present and accept it only after running it through your own God-given conscience, defined by Proverbs as "the lamp of the LORD" (Proverbs 20:27) and by biblical

---

[1]Charlene Altemose, *Why Do Catholics . . .?* (Dubuque, Iowa: BROWN Publishing—ROA Media, 1989)

scholar John MacArthur as "that instinctive sense of right and wrong that produces guilt when violated."[2] I also encourage you to reread any cited biblical passages in your own personal Bible whenever the Holy Spirit prompts you. "Do not despise the words of prophets, but test everything," Paul says in 1 Thessalonians 5:20–21. Before you can use this information to help build and solidify your interfaith relationship, you each must, as Paul also advises, be fully convinced in your own mind (Romans 14:5).

Please try to read this book with an open heart and an open mind. Try to set aside preconceived ideas and prejudices regarding the issues covered in this book. Through doing this, you can take full advantage of the learning and growth opportunities that this book offers, for you as individuals and as a united Christian interfaith couple.

For the purposes of this book, I am discussing relations between traditional Roman Catholics and evangelical Protestants. I do, however, recognize that there are many divisions within Protestantism, whose respective beliefs cannot be fairly addressed in a collective grouping such as this. I am not a theologian and I apologize in advance for any misunderstandings this grouping may cause and encourage you to seek clarification of beliefs from your respective Protestant denomination, if necessary, and from the *Catechism of the Catholic Church* (United States Catholic Conference, 1994, 1997).

Because "faith" is sometimes used interchangeably with "denomination," especially when referring to people of different religions, I use the term "interfaith" throughout this book to refer to a couple of different Christian religions, essentially an interdenominational couple.

It is my hope and prayer that you will be convinced of the integrity and soundness of *United in Heart, Divided in Faith* and that you will find the book's approach to be enlightening and refreshing in the midst of your turmoil. Please read this book together, talk about it, and open your minds and hearts to God's wisdom and guidance. Good luck, and God bless.

Sandy Stanko

---

[2]John MacArthur, *The MacArthur Study Bible* (Nashville: Word Publishing, 1997), 1695.

PREFACE

The Foundation of Faith

I have been crucified with Christ; and it is no longer I who live, but it is Christ who lives in me. And the life I now live in the flesh I live by faith in the Son of God, who loved me and gave himself for me (Galatians 2:19–20).

Before delving into the issues covered in the rest of this book, you both must have a clear understanding of the cornerstone upon which all Christian beliefs are based: faith in the saving power of Jesus Christ. As Christians, both Catholics and Protestants try their best to live their lives based on the teachings of Jesus. In fact, every Catholic-Protestant conflict of belief exists because each denomination is fervently convinced that it is following the precepts established by the true gospel. These convictions stem from the faith that each person has in God, in Jesus, and in the Holy Spirit. Just as Jesus instructed Paul to open the eyes of the Gentiles (Acts 26:18), Jesus uses our faith to open our minds to his teachings and make us wary of conflicts with those teachings. Through this faith, we can accept and follow the truth in our lives, which is the way of Jesus Christ. And in following the truth, our faith also provides us with discernment to evaluate right from wrong.

Your faith is now a crucial element in evaluating issues, gaining wisdom and understanding, making decisions, and exercising discernment within your interfaith relationship.

But what essentially is faith? First and foremost, faith itself is a gift of God's grace, but grace is also necessary for one to accept and use the gift of faith. Hebrews expounds upon the definition of faith, saying that "faith is the assurance of things hoped for, the conviction of things not seen" (Hebrews 11:1). Faith is also "the persuasion of the mind that a certain statement is true. . . . Its primary idea is trust. A thing is true, and therefore worthy of trust."[3] Through faith, we can know that the gospel is truth because we trust in its source, God. Therefore, our faith enables us to accept the saving truths of the gospel, which would seem improbable to our intellect without faith.

Faith is more than just believing in God, for "even the demons believe—and shudder" (James 2:19). Faith is belonging to God, surrendering one's whole being completely to God and being prepared to do his will in your life, as Jesus says in John 15:4: " 'Abide in me as I abide in you. Just as the branch cannot bear fruit by itself unless it abides in the vine, neither can you unless you abide in me.' " With complete submission to Jesus, you imitate the relationship that Jesus has with his Father, including fulfilling God's will as Jesus does: " 'The words that I say to you I do not speak on my own; but the Father who dwells in me does his works. Believe me that I am in the Father and the Father is in me' " (John 14:10–11).

Catholics and Protestants alike agree that one's faith must be a humble faith, in which one depends on and acknowledges the grace of God in all things. Jesus describes this type of humble faith as being like that of a child: " 'Whoever becomes humble like this child is the greatest in the kingdom of heaven' " (Matthew 18:4). And looking at things from a child's perspective makes it easier to see why Jesus has said this. When a child asks for something, he or she expects to receive it, without a doubt. Likewise, when someone tells a child something, he or she accepts it without question. As we grow older, though, we tend to use more "reason" and less pure faith, relying more on ourselves and our intellect and less on God and thus becoming limited in what we can do. Humbling and simplifying our faith makes us more capable of doing for

---

[3]M. G. Easton, *Easton's Bible Dictionary* (1897; Albany, Oreg.: AGES Software, 1997), 423.

Christ what some may view as impossible—walking on water, moving mountains, withering a fig tree, or even making an interfaith relationship work.

Faith is also continuing to trust in God, even when the odds seem stacked against you and your human mind can't comprehend a resolution to your conflict or problem. In Romans 4:17–22, Paul describes how Abraham knew that God has promised him countless descendants (Genesis 15:5), yet "did not weaken in faith when he considered his own body, which was already as good as dead (for he was about a hundred years old), or when he considered the barrenness of Sarah's womb" (Romans 4:19). Consequently, Abraham's faith "was reckoned to him as righteousness" (Romans 4:22; also Genesis 15:6), and Abraham became the father of many nations. Like Abraham, you must continue to have faith that God will work out the difficulties in your lives, including any conflicts within your interfaith relationship.

And just as God made a promise to Abraham in Genesis 15:5, he makes a promise to you in Matthew 21:22: " 'Whatever you ask for in prayer with faith, you will receive.' " What a fabulous promise this is! As you explore the issues presented in this book, keep this promise in your hearts and use your faith as a guide to navigate through the controversial issues that are threatening and weighing down your interfaith relationship. Remember to continuously ask for God's help, through faith. As he promises, he will guide you.

Here's a special prayer to get you started on your journey:

God, we stand before you, humble and confused.
We don't know exactly what your will is for our lives.
We don't even know for sure if you intend for us to be
*   together.*
But we do know that we feel drawn to each other
*   for some reason, by a force outside ourselves*
*   that we truly believe is you.*
Please open our minds and hearts to the understanding that
*   we seek and genuinely need in order to work through the*
*   problems we are having within our interfaith relationship.*

*Help us to submit ourselves to you so willingly and so
openly that you can reach into the very depths of our
souls to remove any prejudices or misunderstandings
that may be clouding our understanding of the truth and
preventing our Christian unity.*

*Guide us in treating each other with respect as we attempt to
discuss heated and controversial topics and please
prevent any of these issues from tearing our relationship
apart. Show us the way out of this deep, dark hole in
which we seem to be trapped.*

*And if it is your will, we ask you to lead us into a Christian
marriage covenant and to bless us with children, which
we also acknowledge are a gift from you.*

We ask all of this in Jesus' most holy name.

Amen.

Part One

EMPHASIZING THE SIMILARITIES IN OUR FAITH

INTRODUCTION

The Need for Unity

*There is one body and one Spirit, just as you were called
to the one hope of your calling, one Lord, one faith, one
baptism, one God and Father of all, who is above all and
through all and in all* (Ephesians 4:4–6).

This first section of *United in Heart, Divided in Faith* presents those
beliefs that Catholics and Protestants hold in common, the core
Christian faith beliefs that form the basis for each religion. All other
beliefs, such as those presented in the next part, are secondary
or auxiliary beliefs and probably are not worth dividing your relationship over.

Oftentimes, though, Catholics and Protestants don't focus on the
beliefs that they have in common but instead argue over the issues that
divide them. Dr. Alan Schreck, professor of theology at the Franciscan
University of Steubenville, Ohio, explains how he believes Satan uses
these divisions to further weaken the Christian church: "One of Satan's
chief strategies to defeat the church is to divide and isolate its members
from one another and thus deprive them of the strength they can receive
from their fellow members of the communion of saints."[4]

---

[4]Alan Schreck, *Catholic and Christian* (Ann Arbor, Mich.: Servant Books, 1984), 154.

These arguments between Catholics and Protestants are unfortunate because not only do they weaken the Christian church, but they also often overshadow the fact that Catholics and Protestants have much more in common than they do in difference.

At the core, Catholics and Protestants are both groups of Christians striving toward the same goal: an eternal relationship with our Savior, Jesus Christ. In his letters, Paul emphasizes that Christians must remain united as they strive to know Christ. Paul tells us in Romans 15:5, "May the God of steadfastness and encouragement grant you to live in harmony with one another, in accordance with Christ Jesus." In 1 Corinthians 1:10, Paul says, "I appeal to you, brothers and sisters, by the name of our Lord Jesus Christ, that all of you be in agreement and that there be no divisions among you, but that you be united in the same mind and the same purpose." And in Philippians 1:27, he says, "Live your life in a manner worthy of the gospel of Christ, so that . . . I will know that you are standing firm in one spirit, striving side by side with one mind for the faith of the gospel." Protestants and Catholics both recite a similar creed, such as the Nicene Creed or the Apostles' Creed, through which they state as a community those core Christian beliefs that they hold in common.

So if the Bible commands all Christians to be united, and Christians profess that they have the same core Christian beliefs, why do divisions still exist? The reason may very well be that, rather than focusing on their common beliefs, both groups focus on those non-core beliefs that differ between Catholics and Protestants. And because many Catholics and Protestants don't thoroughly understand the other group's doctrine—including points about which they agree and disagree— they often judge the other group's religion as a whole based on incomplete or even inaccurate information. Consequently, one group may conclude that the other group is misled in its way of worship and perhaps may not even be Christian. This type of thinking must have started in the very early Christian church, which is why Paul was trying to quell the conflicts and potential divisions with his various appeals.

Introduction

Frequently, simple misunderstandings prevent Catholics and Protestants from seeing that their core beliefs are the same. Gary Hoge, an atheist turned evangelical Protestant turned Catholic, believes that semantics has a lot to do with these misunderstandings: "When it comes to theology, Catholics and Protestants don't speak the same language. Sometimes we use different words to describe the same thing, and sometimes we use the same words to describe different things."[5] A good example of this difference in semantics is the phrase "born again." Protestants often use this phrase to describe the rebirth one goes through when accepting Jesus Christ as his or her personal Savior. And even though Catholics too believe in making a conscious, personal commitment to Jesus Christ, because Catholics don't normally use "born again" to describe this conversion experience, some Protestants may incorrectly believe that Catholics don't actively accept Christ and therefore aren't true Christians.

Another example of misunderstandings resulting from different semantics is the role of works in salvation. Catholics and Protestants both have the same perception of the role of good works in one's life. However, because Catholics officially link works with salvation in official doctrine while Protestants do not, many Protestants have the misunderstanding that Catholics perform good works in an attempt to "earn" their salvation.

Even though divisions do exist between Catholics and Protestants, however, both groups need to remember that the Bible commands us to be united in our core Christian beliefs. This solidarity is especially crucial today against the secular world's obsession with self, greed, lust, and other deadly sins. Christians can exert much power and influence when they present a common, united faith to the secular world. And some Catholics and Protestants do perceive the need for Christian unity, as shown through today's various ecumenical efforts. One of these efforts, initiated by Charles Colson, chairman of Prison Fellowship Ministries, and Father Richard John Neuhaus of the Institute on Religion and Public

---

[5]Gary Hoge, "A Protestant's Guide to the Catholic Church," www.catholicoutlook.com, 1 Aug. 2001. Accessed on 5 Sept. 2002.

Life, was the 1994 controversial and groundbreaking document, "Evangelicals and Catholics Together: The Christian Mission in the Third Millennium," in which a group of evangelical Protestants and Roman Catholics affirm together the core Christian beliefs that they hold in common. Although the authors acknowledge that Catholics and Protestants do have some differing beliefs, the focus of the document is on professing these same, core Christian beliefs:

> As Christ is one, so the Christian mission is one. . . . All who accept Christ as Lord and Savior are brothers and sisters in Christ. Evangelicals and Catholics are brothers and sisters in Christ. We have not chosen one another, just as we have not chosen Christ. He has chosen us, and he has chosen us to be his together (John 15). . . . There is one church because there is one Christ and the church is his body.[6]

The Vatican is also reaching out to other Christians. In an address opening the second session of the Second Vatican Council in 1964, Pope Paul VI asked "pardon of God and of our fellow Christians for the faults committed by Catholics and extend[ed] pardon from the heart for whatever injuries the Church has suffered in the past."[7] The Second Vatican Council also presented the "Decree on Ecumenism," which says in part:

> ". . . there increases from day to day a movement, fostered by the grace of the Holy Spirit, for the restoration of unity among all Christians. Taking part in this movement, which is called ecumenical, are those who invoke the Triune God and confess Jesus as Lord and Savior."[8]

---

[6]Charles Colson et al., "Evangelicals and Catholics Together: The Christian Mission in the Third Millennium," final draft (29 Mar. 1994). This statement appeared in the May 1994 issue of *First Things,* a monthly journal published in New York City by the Institute on Religion and Public Life.

[7]Ronald Lawler, Donald W. Wuerl, and Thomas Comerford Lawler, eds., *The Teaching of Christ* (Huntington, Ind.: Our Sunday Visitor, Inc., 1976), 256.

[8]Alan Schreck, *The Essential Catholic Catechism: A Readable, Comprehensive Catechism of the Catholic Faith* (Ann Arbor, Mich.: Servant Publications, 1999), 142, quoting *Unitatis redintegratio* 1.

But the Catholic Church also recognizes that total Christian unity is beyond the scope of man:

> *"This holy objective—the reconciliation of all Christians in the unity of the one and only Church of Christ—transcends human powers and gifts." That is why we place all our hope "in the prayer of Christ for the Church, in the love of the Father for us, and in the power of the Holy Spirit."* [9]

The part that follows presents the beliefs that Catholics and Protestants hold in common. This part is intended to make you aware of these beliefs, give you a deeper insight into these beliefs, and help you apply these beliefs specifically to your interfaith relationship. This section also strives to clarify any misunderstandings regarding these beliefs that may be a source of division in your relationship.

As you work through this part, remember that, even though one of you is Catholic and one is Protestant, you are both united as Christians: "May the God of steadfastness and encouragement grant you to live in harmony with one another, in accordance with Christ Jesus, so that together you may with one voice glorify the God and Father of our Lord Jesus Christ" (Romans 15:5–6).

---

[9] *Catechism of the Catholic Church* (Liguori, Mo.: Liguori Publications, 1994), 822, quoting *Unitatis redintegratio* 24 §2 .

BELIEF 1

We Believe in God

But Moses said to God, "If I come to the Israelites and say to them, 'The God of your ancestors has sent me to you,' and they ask me, 'What is his name?' what shall I say to them?" God said to Moses, "I am who I am." He said further, "Thus you shall say to the Israelites, 'I am has sent me to you.'" God also said to Moses, "Thus you shall say to the Israelites, 'The Lord, the God of your ancestors, the God of Abraham, the God of Isaac, and the God of Jacob, has sent me to you': This is my name forever, and this my title for all generations" (Exodus 3:13–15).

"We believe in one God the Father Almighty, Maker of heaven and earth." These words, stated in the first lines of the Nicene Creed and the Apostles' Creed, are familiar to both Catholics and Protestants because both groups recite these words in declaration of their common belief in one God, the Father, and the first person in the Holy Trinity or Triune God.

Catholics and Protestants believe that God is the only God because that doctrine is clearly stated in Scripture. Both groups of Christians agree that God firmly and undeniably establishes himself as the only God in the first commandment given to Moses: "I am the Lord your God, who brought you out of the land of Egypt, out of the house of slavery; you shall have no other gods before me" (Exodus 20:2–3). God reiterates himself as sole deity through the prophet Isaiah by saying, "Before me no god was formed, nor shall there be any after me. I, I am the LORD, and besides me there is no savior" (Isaiah 43:10–11), and

"Turn to me and be saved, all the ends of the earth! For I am God, and there is no other" (Isaiah 45:22). And Catholics and Protestants acknowledge that, as the only God, God is omnipotent (all-powerful); omniscient (all-knowing); all-wise; eternal; omnipresent; immutable (unchanging); all-loving; holy; and perfect in goodness, beauty, truth, justice, and mercy.[10]

In addition, Catholics and Protestants teach that God is the eternal Father of Jesus Christ and the spiritual Father of us all. In his position as Father, God fulfills the roles of Creator (Isaiah 40:28), Counselor (Isaiah 9:6), Helper (Psalm 54:4), and Protector (Psalm 121:7), among many others. In fact, as God the Father, God can be whatever you need him to be at a particular time. Recording artist Nichole Nordeman believes that God expressed his willingness to be everything a person would ever need when he referred to himself as "I AM" in Exodus 3:14.[11] Through that seemingly mysterious name, God is saying, "I AM your Friend, I AM your Confidant, I AM your Counselor, I AM your Savior."

Another point upon which Catholics and Protestants agree is that God forbids the practice of idolatry or the worship of other gods. In the commandment given to Moses, God says: "You shall not make for yourself an idol, whether in the form of anything that is in heaven above, or that is on the earth beneath, or that is in the water under the earth. You shall not bow down to them or worship them" (Exodus 20:4–5). Neither Catholics nor Protestants believe in worshipping pagan gods (although some Protestants do feel that Catholics practice idolatry through their devotion to Mary and the other saints and through their use of sacramentals, issues addressed fully in Part 2).

What Catholics and Protestants sometimes forget, however, is that one doesn't have to worship a pagan god in the form of a person or an animal to commit the sin of idolatry. Paul tells us that idolatry can include "whatever in you is earthly: fornication, impurity, passion, evil desire, and greed" (Colossians 3:5). And he acknowledges the detrimental effect that idolatry has even in today's world in 2 Corinthians 4:4:

---

[10]Schreck, *Essential. Catholic Catechism,* 50.

[11]Nichole Nordeman, opening performance for Steven Curtis Chapman's Live Out Loud Tour, 24 Mar. 2002, at Orchard Hills Church, Wexford, Pa.

"[T]he god of this world has blinded the minds of the unbelievers, to keep them from seeing the light of the gospel of the glory of Christ."

In *Praying God's Word,* which talks about eliminating strongholds or "every proud obstacle raised up against the knowledge of God" (2 Corinthians 10:5), writer and teacher Beth Moore elaborates on the idols threatening people today:

> *Virtually every stronghold involves the worship of some kind of idol. For instance, the stronghold of pride is associated with the worship of self. The stronghold of addiction is often associated with the worship of some kind of substance or habit. In one way or another, something else has become "god" in our lives: the object of our chief focus.*[12]

Everyone in one way or another has faced the idolatrous temptations of today's world, and Brian and I are no exception. Likewise, we have experienced the punishment that God promises for all idolaters because, as Moore says, "one sobering thing about the faithfulness of God is that He keeps His promises, even when they are promises of judgment or discipline."[13]

Soon after we were married, Brian and I were thrown into an extremely challenging financial situation. He was unemployed, and my salary was supporting us both but wasn't providing us with enough money to pay all of our expenses. In our financial misery, we fervently prayed for help, and God rescued us in the form of a job for Brian, as he said he would in Psalm 81:7: " 'In distress you called, and I rescued you.' " But it was almost as if, once we got the relief we had asked for, we forgot about God, closing our minds to the warning that God stated so poignantly in the very next verses of the psalm: " 'Hear, O my people, while I admonish you; O Israel, if you would but listen to me! There shall be no strange god among you; you shall not bow down to a foreign god' " (Psalm 81:8–9). We didn't listen and formed a new "god" for ourselves in the form of rich, expensive food. With our new income, we started eating out almost every day, probably spending close to three

[12]Beth Moore, *Praying God's Word* (Nashville, Tenn.: Broadman & Holman Publishers, 2000), 20.
[13]Ibid., 19.

hundred dollars a month on restaurant food at the worst point. And our idolatry led us into a downward spiral through which we ended up in a far worse financial situation than before, accumulating so much debt that we were prevented from buying a house and moving ahead as a family.

Since we hit that bottom, we've tried to refocus our lives on the only true God, but we must continuously and conscientiously resist that idolatrous temptation of frequent restaurant dining. Refocusing on God through prayer and the Bible was our most powerful weapon in combating our idolatrous tendencies.

You must also be careful not to let your interfaith relationship become an idol for either of you, where you are focusing so much energy on it that you lose sight of the God who truly holds the power to make your relationship work. Instead of becoming self-absorbed and turning *from* God, turn *to* God, placing your interfaith relationship into his hands and trusting him to guide you through the problems and conflicts you are having. There is no better time to do this than right now, at the beginning of this book and the journey of discovery that you are embarking on together. Hand over your relationship completely to God, take a deep breath as this burden is lifted from you, and recite these familiar words from Psalm 62:5–8:

> *For God alone my soul waits in silence,*
> *for my hope is from him.*
> *He alone is my rock and my salvation,*
> *my fortress; I shall not be shaken.*
> *On God rests my deliverance and my honor;*
> *my mighty rock, my refuge is in God.*
> *Trust in him at all times, O people;*
> *pour out your heart before him; God is a refuge for us.*

Relationship Builders

- Catholics and Protestants believe in only one, true God.
  Do we both hold this basic Christian belief in one God?
  How have we experienced the presence of God in our individual
      lives?
  In our interfaith relationship?

- Scripture indicates that God can be whatever or whomever we need
  him to be.
  What roles do we need God to take in our interfaith relationship?
      Guide?
      Counselor?
      Confidant?
      Interpreter?
      Mediator?

- God forbids the practice of idolatry, or the worshipping of other
  gods. Idolatry can include a preoccupation with worldly influences.
  Are there any idols that either of us holds in higher esteem than
      God?
  How might these inhibit not only our personal growth with God
      but also the growth of our relationship?

- Becoming obsessed or blindly focused on resolving the religious
  differences between you can also turn your relationship into a type
  of idolatry.
  Are we concentrating so hard on thinking of ways to make our
      relationship work that we are forgetting to rely on God for help?
  Can we agree to turn our relationship problems over to God for
      resolution, as Psalm 55:22 tells us to do: "Cast your burden on
      the Lord, and he will sustain you; he will never permit the
      righteous to be moved"?

BELIEF 2

We Believe in Jesus Christ

*[I]f you confess with your lips that Jesus is Lord and believe
in your heart that God raised him from the dead, you will be
saved* (Romans 10:9).

Christianity is one of the world's dominant religions, with more than
two billion members worldwide in more than a thousand denominations and thousands more in nondenominational Christian churches.
So many denominations exist because the facets and nuances of
Christianity have been picked apart and debated by scholars around the
globe. And some of these debates have probably found their way into
your interfaith relationship as well. Ironically, in spite of the many
complexities that man has infused into the practice of Christianity, the
foundation of the religion is strikingly simple: belief in Jesus Christ as
fully God, fully man, and Savior of the world.

"Have you accepted Jesus Christ as your personal Savior?" is a
question often posed by Protestants to both Catholics and nonbelievers.
Catholics are often confused by this question because they view faith as
a growth process through sanctification that begins at baptism rather
than as a single, identifiable commitment, causing confusion and
misunderstandings in Catholic-Protestant discussions. In spite of the
different ways in which they may describe their conversion experience,
both Catholics and Protestants believe in Jesus Christ as God, man, and
Savior. This crucial, foundational Christian belief should also be an
important focal point of unity for your interfaith relationship.

Through Scripture, we know that Jesus has always existed alongside God and the Holy Spirit as the second member of the Holy Trinity or Triune God. In Colossians 1:15–16, Paul tells us about Jesus' role in creation: "He is the image of the invisible God, the firstborn of all creation; for in him all things in heaven and on earth were created, things visible and invisible, whether thrones or dominions or rulers or powers—all things have been created through him and for him." There is also evidence of Jesus in the Old Testament, before his human birth. In Joshua 5:13–15, Joshua meets a man who identifies himself as " 'commander of the army of the LORD' " (Joshua 5:14). Joshua falls down in worship before this man, and the man did not correct him for doing so, as an angel would have (see Revelation 19:10), indicating that this man was God, most likely Christ.

Jesus' role took on another dimension, however, when God recognized the toil sin was taking on the world. Since the original sin committed by Adam and Eve, mankind had been encased in sin and suffering death as the ultimate penalty of sin. Because of his infinite love for man, God wanted to reconcile us to himself. The only way that he could have reconciliation within the law that he himself had established, however, was to have a perfect human bear his wrath for all of mankind's sin. Because no human being was perfect, God knew he had to incarnate his son to be "the Savior of the world" (1 John 4:14). Therefore, God selected Mary, a woman, a virgin, from among his chosen people, Israel, in the line of David to bear his son, thus fulfilling the prophesies of Isaiah 7:14 and Jeremiah 23:5. God sent the angel Gabriel to Mary to explain that the "Holy Spirit will come upon you, and the power of the Most High will overshadow you; therefore the child to be born will be holy; he will be called Son of God" (Luke 1:35). Mary agreed to God's plan, and Jesus was conceived. Therefore, Catholics and Protestants agree that Jesus was both fully God and fully man:

> *Let the same mind be in you that was in Christ Jesus, who, though he was in the form of God, did not regard equality with God as something to be exploited, but emptied himself, taking*

the form of a slave, being born in human likeness. And being found in human form, he humbled himself and became obedient to the point of death—even death on a cross (Philippians 2:5–8).

Jesus came to earth to teach biblical truths and ultimately to die for our sins at Calvary. Through Christ's one and perfect sacrifice, the salvation that God originally intended for man was again available to those who believe in Christ. Jesus himself says:

"For God so loved the world that he gave his only Son, so that everyone who believes in him may not perish but may have eternal life. Indeed, God did not send the Son into the world to condemn the world, but in order that the world might be saved through him. Those who believe in him are not condemned; but those who do not believe are condemned already, because they have not believed in the name of the only Son of God" (John 3:16–18).

Catholics and Protestants also believe that, three days after he died, Jesus rose from the dead, appearing to his disciples as the resurrected Christ. Forty days after his resurrection, in the presence of his disciples, Jesus ascended into heaven to the right hand of God (Ephesians 1:20). As the disciples gazed heavenward, two men dressed in white said to them, " 'Men of Galilee, why do you stand looking up toward heaven? This Jesus, who has been taken up from you into heaven, will come in the same way as you saw him go into heaven' " (Acts 1:11). Christ's second coming is another belief that Catholics and Protestants hold in common: "[S]o Christ, having been offered once to bear the sins of many, will appear a second time, not to deal with sin, but to save those who are eagerly waiting for him" (Hebrews 9:28).

During his ministry on earth, Jesus taught many, many biblical truths. These truths are directly applicable to your interfaith relationship, and some of them are presented below. As you read through them, think of how they pertain to your relationship and how they can help to establish and solidify the Christian unity you are seeking. I also encourage you to delve into Jesus' teachings yourself to see what other insights God can give you to apply to your relationship struggles.

Biblical truth: Jesus says, " 'I am the way, and the truth, and the life. No one comes to the Father except through me. If you know me, you will know my Father also. From now on you do know him and have seen him' " (John 14:6–7). By inviting Jesus—who is the way—into your relationship, you set the course of your relationship along a "path of righteousness [where] there is life" (Proverbs 12:28) and establish Christ as your navigator through the twists and turns your relationship is bound to take. Through him who is truth, you will have access to infallible and unwavering truths so that you can build your relationship not on sand but on rock (Matthew 7:24–27). A solid, stable foundation in Christ will make your relationship strong, able to withstand outside pressures from other people, demons, and even your own inhibitions and weaknesses. And by acknowledging and accepting that Jesus is life, you can each accept God's gift of salvation and invite Jesus to breathe life and strength into your Christian interfaith relationship.

Biblical truth: " 'Believe me that I am in the Father and the Father is in me. . . . I will do whatever you ask in my name, so that the Father may be glorified in the Son. If in my name you ask me for anything, I will do it' " (John 14:11, 13–14). Jesus confirms here that he is God and promises you that, as God, he will be your strongest ally in working through the difficulties in your relationship. Jesus also promises access to the wisdom of the Father for guidance in your relationship: " '[N]o one knows the Son except the Father, and no one knows the Father except the Son and anyone to whom the Son chooses to reveal him' " (Matthew 11:27). When you are working through the issues in your relationship, remember to pray for Christ's divine wisdom and read the Scriptures for guidance.

Biblical truth: " 'Whoever does the will of my Father in heaven is my brother and sister and mother' " (Matthew 12:50). Scripture tells us that we are "children of God, and if children, then heirs, heirs of God and joint heirs with Christ" (Romans 8:16–17). Sometimes, in the midst of volatile Catholic-Protestants debates, it is easy to forget that we are all Christians and therefore brothers and sisters and joint heirs, all "members of the household of God" (Ephesians 2:19). Remember, as Christians, you hold the same core Christian beliefs. And as Christians, you need to respect the other person's beliefs, even those about which you disagree. You will get so much farther in establishing a unified relationship through mutual respect rather than trying to undermine or disprove the beliefs of the other person.

Relationship Builders

- Believing in Jesus Christ as fully man, fully God, and Savior is the foundation of Christianity.
  Have we both consciously accepted Christ as our personal Savior?
  Have we also accepted this foundational belief of Christianity as the foundation and focal point of our interfaith relationship?

- Jesus has always existed as God with God the Father and God the Holy Spirit.
  What can we learn about trust—of God and of each other—through Jesus' eternal dependence on his Father?

- Jesus' role is unique as God because he became human. And as human, Jesus personally experienced the wide range of emotions that we experience.
  How could Jesus' first-hand experiences as a human provide us with valuable insight into working through the emotions and other inhibitors of a harmonious, unified Christian relationship?

- Through his ultimate sacrifice, Jesus demonstrated his love for mankind by again making salvation possible for all men.
  We rely on Christ's love for our salvation. How can we also rely on his love, and the messages of what he taught through love, for support and guidance within our interfaith relationship?

BELIEF 3

We Believe in the Holy Spirit

[T]he Spirit searches everything, even the depths of God. For what human being knows what is truly human except the human spirit that is within? So also no one comprehends what is truly God's except the Spirit of God. Now we have received not the spirit of the world, but the Spirit that is from God, so that we may understand the gifts bestowed on us by God (1 Corinthians 2:10–12).

Along with believing in God the Father and God the Son, Catholics and Protestants believe in God the Holy Spirit, the third person in the Holy Trinity or Triune God. Catholic and Protestant theologians and writers agree that, of the three persons in the Trinity, the Holy Spirit is the least understood. The Holy Spirit was the last person in the Trinity to be revealed by God, yet he is the most intimately involved in our initial conversion and development as Christians. The Holy Spirit is who makes it possible for Christians to accept Christ and profess that he is Lord and Savior (1 Corinthians 12:3).

The Holy Spirit was part of God since the beginning of time and did indeed help create the universe and man (Genesis 1:2). In Acts 5:3–4, where Peter admonishes a man named Ananias from withholding money from God, Scripture establishes that the Holy Spirit is indeed God: " 'Ananias,' Peter asked, 'why has Satan filled your heart to lie to the Holy Spirit and to keep back part of the proceeds of the land? . . . You did not lie to us but to God!' " The Holy Spirit was present in the Old Testament but acted in a limited capacity, coming upon men temporarily for special purposes and then retreating. It wasn't until Jesus died for our sins and established the new covenant that the Holy Spirit was free to dwell in the hearts of believers permanently. "God's love has been poured into our hearts through the Holy Spirit that has been given to us" (Romans 5:5).

The Holy Spirit has many roles in the lives of Christians, including filling us with God's power and righteousness, guiding us in all truth, and revealing to us the will of God the Father for our lives. Another important role of the Holy Spirit dwelling in our hearts is to bestow spiritual gifts "to each one individually just as the Spirit chooses" (1 Corinthians 12:11) "for the common good" (1 Corinthians 12:7). Christians believe that each person has at least one spiritual gift, others more. In 1 Corinthians, Paul lists some of the forms that these spiritual gifts could take:

> To one is given through the Spirit the utterance of wisdom, and to another the utterance of knowledge according to the same Spirit, to another faith by the same Spirit, to another gifts of healing by the one Spirit, to another the working of miracles, to another prophecy, to another the discernment of spirits, to another various kinds of tongues, to another the interpretation of tongues (1 Corinthians 12:8–10).

Paul emphasizes that, although the gifts are different, they are from the same Spirit who baptizes all Christians into one body (1 Corinthians 12:13). The Holy Spirit distributes the gifts in such a way as to promote the unity of the body of Christians, "that there may be no dissension within the body, but the members may have the same care for one another" (1 Corinthians 12:25).

The Holy Spirit's intention for Christian unity is something to keep in mind as you try to work out the conflicts you are having in your inter-faith relationship. Schreck believes that many problems among

Christians today may result from people not understanding or recognizing their Spirit-given gifts—and the gifts given to others.[14] Perhaps this rings true in your relationship. You may be so self-centered on your "correct" beliefs that you are refusing to open your mind to the beliefs, perspectives, and other gifts brought to the relationship by your partner. Or maybe you are gifted in explaining your beliefs and tend to drone on in oratory without giving your partner a chance to respond. Conversely, you may be more gifted in listening than speaking and so tend to be the quiet one in the relationship and not verbalize the beliefs and views you hold inside. In order to make your relationship work, you need to identify the spiritual gifts with which you are each blessed and pray for God's guidance in how to use these gifts complementarily to work through the issues in your relationship.

God is ready and willing to pour his Spirit into you, but you must also be willing recipients. Just as the Holy Spirit came upon the apostles for the first time at Pentecost (Acts 2:4), the Spirit can come upon each of you when you pray to "be filled with the Spirit" (Ephesians 5:18). Having the Spirit of God within you can help you grow more Christlike and make you more resistant to the temptations all around. And when the Holy Spirit dwells within you, it is something you can surely feel. He will prompt you, lead you, and let you know, sometimes in seemingly insignificant ways, that he is present. You will also see positive results of decisions you make when relying upon the guidance of the Holy Spirit.

When the Spirit is working within you, he is able to bear his fruit: love, charity, joy, peace, patience, kindness, goodness, generosity, faithfulness, chastity, modesty, gentleness, and self-control (Galatians 5:22–23).[15] And you need all of these attributes to make your interfaith relationship healthy and strong. Pray that God's Spirit will bear this fruit inside you and show you how to apply this fruit to your interfaith relationship.

---

[14]Schreck, *Essential Catholic Catechism,* 210.

[15]*CCC,* 1832.

Relationship Builders

- Catholics and Protestants both believe in the Holy Spirit, the third person in the Holy Trinity or Triune God and consubstantial with the Father and the Son.
  Do we both believe in the Holy Spirit?
  Do we believe he is part of one God and equal to God the Father and Jesus the Son?

- The Holy Spirit is the one who distributes spiritual gifts to all Christians.
  What gifts has the Spirit given to each of us?
  How can these gifts help to promote unity within our interfaith relationship, along with promoting unity among all Christians?

- The Holy Spirit can make his presence known in our lives through both large and small ways.
  In what ways has the Spirit manifested himself in our lives?
  Can we see the Spirit's influence in our interfaith relationship? Why or why not?
  Have we asked that our relationship be "filled with the Spirit"?

- Like a fertile tree, the Holy Spirit will also bear fruit within faithful Christians.
  How can we cultivate the fruit of the Spirit in our lives?
  How can we apply this fruit to our interfaith relationship to help it grow in strength and holiness?

BELIEF 4

We Believe in the Holy Trinity or Triune God

[F]or through [Jesus] both of us have access in one Spirit to the Father (Ephesians 2:18).

Along with believing in God the Father, Jesus the Son, and the Holy Spirit, Christians also believe that these three persons are all part of one God, called the Holy Trinity or Triune God. The *Catechism of the Catholic Church* calls the belief in the Holy Trinity "the central mystery of Christian faith and life."[16] It is a concept so beyond the grasp of human understanding that it can only be conveyed through divine revelation and accepted through genuine faith. But it is only through belief in the Holy Trinity that one can accept the other teachings of the Christian faith, including the core belief that Jesus as the divine Son took the form of human flesh through the Holy Spirit for the purpose of dying on the cross as a perfect human sacrifice for the appeasement of God the Father.

The essence of the Holy Trinity is that each member of the Trinity—the Father, the Son, and the Holy Spirit—is completely and wholly God, and each is completely and wholly within the others. And at the same time that the Father, Son, and Holy Spirit are one God, they are three persons, distinct from the others only in their relationship to

---

[16]*CCC*, 234.

41

each of the others. "The Father is always the Father to the eternal Son, who is ever His only-begotten and uncreated Son. The Holy Spirit lives always as the Person who expresses the eternal love that binds the Father and the Son."[17] Moreover, God the Father is the supreme authority, while Jesus is the submissive Son who is exalted by the Father. And the Holy Spirit, while the Spirit of both of them, can also be thought of as being the love between them that is itself so powerful that it is God.

Interestingly, there is no explicit reference to "Trinity" or "Triune God" in the Bible. Yet, biblical evidence still exists to support this core doctrine. The existence of multiple persons in one God is suggested in such Old Testament passages as Genesis 1:26, where God speaks using plural pronouns: "Then God said, 'Let us make humankind in our image, according to our likeness.' " In Acts 20:28 of the New Testament, Paul implies the existence of the Holy Trinity when he says, "Keep watch over yourselves and over all the flock, of which the Holy Spirit has made you overseers, to shepherd the church of God that he obtained with the blood of his own Son." Another New Testament reference to the Trinity is when Jesus sends his apostles out for the Great Commission to baptize " 'in the name of the Father and of the Son and of the Holy Spirit' " (Matthew 28:19). And another is in Paul's closing to 2 Corinthians: "The grace of the Lord Jesus Christ, the love of God, and the communion of the Holy Spirit be with all of you" (2 Corinthians 13:13).

Although no exact comparisons can be made to the mystery of the Holy Trinity, aspects of this perfect relationship can help you build and strengthen your interfaith relationship. Although different, the Father, Son, and Holy Spirit live as one in perfect harmony within the Holy Trinity, a beautiful example of unified diversity. Each supports the other in a perfect balance, God in authority, Christ in submission, and the Spirit as their love. As two different people seeking unity as one, you can also model your relationship after this divine example, submitting to one another in balance, not fighting for authority or control. Paul states the necessity of this mutual submission in Ephesians 5:21, when

---

[17] R. Lawler, Wuerl, and T. C. Lawler, *Teaching of Christ,* 179.

he advises husbands and wives to "be subject to one another out of reverence for Christ."

While the relationship of those within the Holy Trinity is an example of unity for your relationship, the Trinity as God is at the same time absolutely necessary in establishing and maintaining that unity. In describing how he wants all Christians to be united, Jesus describe the oneness with the Trinity that you will have if you enter into a marriage covenant with each other and with God:

> *I ask not only on behalf of these [disciples], but also on behalf of those who will believe in me through their word, that they may all be one. As you, Father, are in me and I am in you, may they also be in us, so that the world may believe that you have sent me. The glory that you have given me I have given them, so that they may be one, as we are one, I in them and you in me, that they may become completely one, so that the world may know that you have sent me and have loved them even as you have loved me* (John 17:20–23).

In marriage, you will be united with your spouse and with God, the unity of you three reflecting the triplicate nature of the Holy Trinity. And within this covenant, God promises you will also have the support of the Holy Trinity: "Christ is the head of every man, and the husband is the head of his wife, and God is the head of Christ" (1 Corinthians 11:3).

Furthermore, when you live in unity as husband and wife, any children you may have, borne out of your love, reflects the love, the Holy Spirit, that continuously flows between the Father and the Son.

Relationship Builders

* The Holy Trinity or Triune God comprises God the Father, God the Son, and God the Holy Spirit, three distinct persons joined as one God.
  Have we both accepted this central Christian mystery of the Holy Trinity?

- Although Scripture doesn't refer to the Trinity or Triune God using these terms, Catholics and Protestants both agree that this doctrine is undeniably contained within Scripture.

  Since the names "Trinity" and "Triune God" do not appear in Scripture, is it more difficult for either of us to accept this Christian principle? Why or why not?

  Might our perceptions make it easier to discuss some of the disputed Catholic beliefs presented in Part 2, which Catholics believe are contained within Scripture, although they are often not explicitly stated?

- The Trinity can provide you with a divine model for your relationship.

  In what ways can we strengthen and improve our interfaith relationship by using the example of the Holy Trinity?

  What traits of the Trinity could each of us reflect specifically?

- The Trinity is also integral in establishing the Christian unity you are seeking, especially within a marriage covenant.

  Can we pray for the Holy Trinity to bind with us now as a couple, to start a work of conversion from self to selfless unity, a relationship that will be sealed eternally with our marriage covenant with God?

BELIEF 5

We Believe in Salvation by Grace Through Faith

Although you have not seen him, you love him; and even though you do not see him now, you believe in him and rejoice with an indescribable and glorious joy, for you are receiving the outcome of your faith, the salvation of your souls (1 Peter 1:8–9).

"When we first met, I asked Sandy if she was saved," says Brian. "Her puzzled response of 'I believe in Jesus. Is that the same thing?' made me question whether or not she was truly going to heaven, and whether or not I wanted to be involved with someone who may not be saved."

In this conversation, Brian and I were unknowingly comparing apples and caramel apples, where the core was the same but the outside presentation was a bit different. Both Brian and I were "saved" by the Bible's definition, but we both became confused when he used this word to describe our conversion while I did not. The different words and phrases used by Catholics and Protestants regarding salvation often lead to misunderstandings such as this and may have even caused some discord within your interfaith relationship.

In discussing salvation, it may be helpful to understand why salvation is needed and to understand its source, the grace of God.

Before Adam and Eve sinned, God planned for man to live eternally in peace and harmony with him in paradise. Man's sin brought death into the world and caused God to say to Adam, " 'You are dust, and to dust you shall return' " (Genesis 3:19) before banishing him and Eve from the garden of Eden forever.

However, God in his infinite goodness wanted to reconcile his bond with man, and the only way to do that was through the sacrifice and suffering of the only perfect man, Jesus Christ: "It was fitting that God, for whom and through whom all things exist, in bringing many children to glory, should make the pioneer of their salvation perfect through sufferings" (Hebrews 2:10). Paul elaborates in Romans 5:18: "Therefore just as one man's trespass led to condemnation for all, so one man's act of righteousness leads to justification and life for all." Jesus died for every person's sins, reconciling man's bond with God and again enabling people to enter into heaven with God, or have salvation.

Both Catholics and Protestants agree that salvation is a free gift from the grace of God bought for us by the suffering, death, and resurrection of Jesus Christ. We don't deserve salvation, nor can we "earn" it in any way, including earning it through our faith. But through faith alone, which is itself also a gift of God's grace, we can consciously accept God's gift of eternal salvation, along with the justification that wipes away our sins and prepares us to live with God forever in glory.

When a person chooses to accept God's gift of salvation, he or she becomes a Christian, a new person: "[I]f anyone is in Christ, there is a new creation: everything old has passed away; see, everything has become new!" (2 Corinthians 5:17). The way in which a person becomes a Christian through accepting salvation is what the Bible refers to as being "born from above" or "born again." Jesus himself said a person must be born again in order to have eternal life in heaven: " 'Very truly, I tell you, no one can see the kingdom of God without being born from above' " (John 3:3). Catholics and Protestants alike believe in the necessity of becoming a new person in Christ, even though Protestants will use the phrase "born again" more often than Catholics to describe the conversion experience. While Catholics and some Protestants believe infants receive justification and salvation at baptism through the faith of their parents, both denominations also believe it is necessary to make a mature, adult commitment to Jesus Christ as one's Savior. (See *Belief 10: We Believe in the Importance of Baptism* beginning on page 71 for more discussion about similarities and differences regarding baptism.)

Some Protestants also have the impression that Catholics try to earn their salvation through good works and participation in the Catholic sacraments. However, Catholics, like Protestants, believe that faith in one's salvation produces works. Works cannot produce salvation, as Paul emphasizes in Ephesians 2:8–9: "For by grace you have been saved through faith, and this is not your own doing; it is the gift of God—not the result of works, so that no one may boast." (See *Belief 7: We Believe in Performing Good Works to Outwardly Reflect Our Inner Faith* on page 53.)

Catholics also genuinely believe that God established the Catholic sacraments as the laws of the new covenant. Therefore, participating in them is seen as obeying God's law because one is saved, not as a means of earning salvation, supporting Scripture such as Romans 3:28, which says, "For we hold that a person is justified by faith apart from works prescribed by the law." (See *Difference 6: Sacraments* on page 141.)

As with any gift, salvation can be accepted or rejected. Each person—Catholic and Protestant alike—must actively choose to accept this gift. Schreck says, "Unfortunately, some Catholics have neglected the importance of this conscious, personal commitment to Jesus Christ. Catholics sometimes assume that persons who are baptized, attend Mass, and receive the sacraments regularly have obviously accepted Jesus Christ as the Lord and Savior of their lives."[18] Consequently, the Catholic Church in recent years has emphasized the conversion of all people—including Catholics—to a personal faith based upon the saving work of Jesus Christ.

Regardless of how they describe their conversion, Catholics and Protestants must make a deliberate decision to accept Jesus as their

[18]Schreck, *Catholic and Christian,* 23.

personal Savior and receive the gift of eternal salvation through faith that he has promised each one of us by his grace.

Relationship Builders

* Salvation was necessary for man to live eternally with God due to the original sin committed by Adam and Eve.
  The conflicts we are experiencing in our interfaith relationship are directly related to the sin unleashed by Adam and Eve. How could the promise of salvation, offered by God to overcome sin, also help us to overcome obstacles in our relationship?

* The suffering, death, and resurrection of Jesus Christ are what have earned us salvation.
  Do we agree that salvation is a free gift willingly offered to us by God out of his grace and not because of anything we have done to deserve it?
  Do we agree that works or anything else we might do ourselves won't earn us salvation?

* We can only be saved through faith alone, a gift of God's grace.
  Do we understand the source of our faith—God—which enables us to accept God's gift of salvation?
  What are some steps we could take to cultivate our faith?
  How could an increase in personal faith help our interfaith relationship?

* A Christian is someone who has consciously accepted Jesus Christ as his or her personal Savior, regardless of the terminology used to describe the experience. Catholics and some Protestants also believe that infants are initiated into the Christian faith through the sacrament of Baptism when they are presented by their parents.
  Since we are both adults, have we each taken the simple step to consciously accept Christ as our Savior, in spite of whether we attend church regularly, receive the sacraments, or do anything else we think should have "showed" God that we are Christians?

BELIEF 6

We Believe in Eternal Life

Blessed be the God and Father of our Lord Jesus Christ! By his great mercy he has given us a new birth into a living hope through the resurrection of Jesus Christ from the dead, and into an inheritance that is imperishable, undefiled, and unfading, kept in heaven for you, who are being protected by the power of God through faith for a salvation ready to be revealed in the last time (1 Peter 1:3–5).

When he created Adam and Eve, God intended for them and their descendants to live in harmony with him forever. But because of man's sin, death entered the world and prevented men from having this eternal unity with God. It wasn't until the death and resurrection of Jesus Christ that eternal life was again possible for men, "for since death came through a human being, the resurrection of the dead has also come through a human being; for as all die in Adam, so all will be made alive in Christ" (1 Corinthians 15:21–22). Catholics and Protestants are united in the belief that, through Jesus, they can have eternal life in heaven with God, which was preached by Jesus as the will and commandment of God (John 6:40, 12:50).

As was presented in *Belief 5: We Believe in Salvation by Grace Through Faith,* Catholics and Protestants both believe that the salvation that results in eternal life is a free, unmerited gift, available to anyone who believes in Jesus Christ as Savior. Jesus himself says repeatedly that believing in him is the way to eternal life: " 'This is indeed the will of my Father, that all who see the Son and believe in him may have eternal life' " (John 6:40) and " 'Very truly, I tell you, whoever believes has eternal life' " (John 6:47).

Most Christians believe that eternal life begins in this life, when one accepts this gift of salvation through Christ, either at baptism (via the faith of one's parents for an infant or via one's personal faith for an adult) or through a formal acceptance of Christ as a mature Christian. At this moment, a person becomes "a new creation" (2 Corinthians 5:17), and the process of sanctification (becoming more Christlike) begins. In his conversation with the Samaritan woman at the well, Jesus compares the sanctification process to " 'a spring of water gushing up to eternal life' " (John 4:14). Sanctification continues throughout a person's life, being completed at death when a faithful Christian is welcomed into eternal life in heaven. (Catholics teach that sanctification can continue even after death when some believers may have to undergo spiritual purification in purgatory before entering heaven. See *Difference 9: Purgatory* on page 167.)

Although no one knows for sure, the Bible provides some information about what eternal life with God will be like. John describes the pure bliss that the saved will experience in God's presence in heaven, describing in Revelation 21:3–4 a voice he heard saying, " 'See, the home of God is among mortals. He will dwell with them as their God; they will be his peoples, and God himself will be with them; he will wipe every tear from their eyes. Death will be no more; mourning and crying and pain will be no more, for the first things have passed away.' " And Jesus says that there are " 'many dwelling places' " (John 14:2) in his Father's house, one of which he has prepared for each believer. We don't know much more beyond these references. Ironically, what we do know for certain about heaven is how much we really don't know, that our limited human consciousness can't even comprehend the happiness that waits in eternal life: " '[N]o eye has seen, nor ear heard, nor the human heart conceived, what God has prepared for those who love him' " (1 Corinthians 2:9).

But the Bible also reminds us that the road to eternal life is not easy. " 'Strive to enter through the narrow door,' " Jesus says in Luke 13:24. " 'For many, I tell you, will try to enter and will not be able.' " Accepting Jesus' gift of eternal life means that you will need to take up your cross and follow him (Mark 8:34), which may include pursuing your interfaith relationship against one or both of your families' wishes. However, Jesus says that you must ultimately listen to and obey his will for your lives, even if it means going against the will of others: " 'And everyone who has left houses or brothers or sisters or father or mother or children or fields, for my name's sake, will receive a hundredfold, and will inherit eternal life' " (Matthew 19:29). (For guidance on handling your families' objections to your interfaith relationship, see page 236, *Discussion 7: How Do We Respond to Questions, Comments, and Pressures From Our Families and Friends?*)

Relationship Builders

- The eternal life originally intended for all men was lost through the sin of Adam and Eve and then regained through the death and resurrection of Jesus Christ.
  Through trusting in Jesus, we have the hope of eternal life.
  How can we translate this hope—and trust—into other areas of our lives, specifically our interfaith relationship?

- With acceptance of salvation, which leads to eternal life, a person's sanctification begins.
  How can our relationship help each of us to grow individually in sanctification?
  Are there any ways in which our relationship inhibits our spiritual growth?

- Little detail is known about what eternal life will be like.
  Have we thought about eternal life or instead been too focused on the present issues of our relationship?
  How might expanding our vision help to alleviate any current pressures on our relationship?

- Accepting Jesus' call may mean opposing some of your family.
  *In what ways do we feel that we may be forsaking our families
  through pursuing this relationship?*
  *Are we each willing to oppose our families' wishes, if necessary,
  for the sake of our relationship?*

BELIEF 7

We Believe in Performing Good Works to Outwardly Reflect Our Inner Faith

How does God's love abide in anyone who has the world's goods and sees a brother or sister in need and yet refuses help? Little children, let us love, not in word or speech, but in truth and action. And by this we will know that we are from the truth (1 John 3:17–19).

Nine months before our scheduled wedding, Brian and I had a fight. Not just one of those little couple squabbles but a big blowup that pretty much called off our wedding temporarily. And to be honest, I don't even remember what started the fight; I just remember hurling words (and thankfully, nothing else!) at each other. What really sent me over the edge, though, was when Brian, out of the blue, said, "And you Catholics believe you can earn your salvation through works, and I can't handle that!"

"What?" I remember yelling back. Where did that come from? Not to mention that I knew it wasn't even true. I later discovered that my husband is the type of person who lets things accumulate inside him, only to erupt all together during some future volatile incident. Obviously, his belief that Catholics attempt to earn their salvation through good works had been festering inside him for a long time.

And my husband isn't the only Protestant to have had this perception. The role of works in justification and salvation is an issue that has been vigorously debated between Catholics and Protestants, and that may not be clearly understood by either denomination.

It is true that Catholics believe that good works have a place in justification and salvation. Catholics believe in the primacy and necessity of faith alone, a gift of God's grace, for justification and salvation. Catholics also assert, however, that one must perform works, not the works of the law condemned by Paul in Romans 3:28, but works of Christian charity and love flowing from faith, as advocated by Jesus in Luke 11:42. A person's works are supposed to reflect his or her justification and salvation, not to earn either.

Catholics believe that only through a genuine faith can a person accept justification and salvation. (This includes the Catholic belief that parents' genuine faith can accept justification and salvation for their children at baptism.) This faith—by the inherent quality of being genuine—will unequivocally produce good works. Therefore, Catholics say that to have justification and salvation, one must perform these works of charity because without the type of genuine faith that will, by its nature, produce works, one cannot be justified or saved. In Romans 4:9–12, Paul speaks about how Abraham received a circumcision "as a seal of the righteousness that he had by faith while he was still uncircumcised" (Romans 4:11). Abraham didn't receive the faith because he was circumcised; his circumcision was a sign of his faith. Likewise, Catholics don't think about being saved as a result of their works; they believe their works are a sign of their faith.

Protestants usually have a problem with official Catholic doctrine saying that works have a place in justification and salvation because they believe in faith alone for both justification and salvation. However, even though Protestants don't directly link works with salvation, they hold the same belief as Catholics in the necessity of living one's inner faith through various good works, including witnessing and acts of charity. In his devotional *Unto the Hills,* well-known evangelist Billy Graham says:

> *Once we are saved—God expects us—in fact He commands us—to not be hearers of the Word only, but doers as well. Works, when we are in Christ, are an extension of Christ's ministry. In fact, works are not ends in themselves, but they demonstrate God's love toward others so that they will know God loves them and so that they will desire to learn about God's provision for their greatest needs.*[19]

Support for living one's faith through good works is found from writers throughout the Bible, including the writer of 1 John who told us to "love—in truth and action" (1 John 3:18) and Paul, who advises us to have "compassion, kindness, humility, meekness, and patience" (Colossians 3:12). James tells us, "[B]e doers of the word, and not merely hearers who deceive themselves" (James 1:22) and "[F]aith by itself, if it has no works, is dead" (James 2:17). Through his letters to Timothy, Paul also explains that we should be "rich in good works" (1 Timothy 6:18) and speaks about the usefulness of Scripture in making "everyone who belongs to God . . . proficient, equipped for every good work" (2 Timothy 3:17).

Jesus himself speaks about the necessity of living one's faith through works in the book of Matthew where he compares the yield of a person's life with a tree that does or does not bear fruit, saying, " 'Every tree that does not bear good fruit is cut down and thrown into the fire. Thus you will know them by their fruits' " (Matthew 7:19–20). Following this story in Matthew, Jesus says, " 'Not everyone who says to me, "Lord, Lord," will enter the kingdom of heaven, but only the one who does the will of my Father in heaven' " (Matthew 7:21).

---

[19]Billy Graham, *Unto the Hills* (Dallas: Word Publishing, 1996), 153.

Also in Matthew, Jesus describes to his disciples those who will receive their heavenly inheritance:

"[F]or I was hungry and you gave me food, I was thirsty and you gave me something to drink, I was a stranger and you welcomed me, I was naked and you gave me clothing, I was sick and you took care of me, I was in prison and you visited me." (Matthew 25:35–36)

There is also evidence throughout the Bible that we will be accountable for our works, both good and bad. In speaking of the Babylonians through Jeremiah, the Lord says, "I will repay them according to their deeds and the work of their hands" (Jeremiah 25:14). In addition, Paul says in Romans 2:6, "For he will repay according to each one's deeds," and also says in 2 Corinthians 5:10, "For all of us must appear before the judgment seat of Christ, so that each may receive recompense for what has been done in the body, whether good or evil." And in Revelation 20:12, John describes how "the dead were judged according to their works, as recorded in the books."

Catholics and Protestants both believe it is through works of love and charity that we can grow in righteousness and sanctification, becoming more Christlike ourselves and, concurrently, enriching and building the whole body of Christ. (See also *Belief 13: We Believe in Evangelization* on page 88.)

It is also worth reiterating that neither Catholics nor Protestants profess that good works, devoid of faith, will bring them salvation. Jesus makes this point in Luke 18:9–14 through a parable in which a Pharisee thanks God that he is not like other men because he fasts and tithes. However, because his works were meant to exult himself and were not borne out of a genuine, humble faith in God, the Pharisee was not justified before God.

Sometimes, Protestants see Catholics participating in rituals such as the Catholic sacraments and argue that Catholics believe that merely participating in the sacraments, another form of "work," is earning them salvation. No doubt there are abuses of the sacraments by Catholics who premeditatedly engage in sin, thinking that after the sin, they only need to participate in a sacrament such as Reconciliation (Confession) in order to be forgiven. Even though some Catholics behave this way, however, approaching the sacraments with this attitude, without genuine, humble faith and remorse, is blasphemy and is not advocated nor tolerated by the Catholic Church. (More about the Catholic sacraments will be covered in *Difference 7: Catholic Sacraments Described* on page 146.)

The difference, then, between Catholics and Protestants regarding the role of works in salvation is that works have a place in salvation in official Catholic doctrine; they do not in official Protestant doctrine. However, Protestants, like Catholics, do believe in the necessity of performing good works that outwardly reflect their inner faith to others and to God. As Jesus himself says in Matthew 5:16, " 'Let your light shine before others, so that they may see your good works and give glory to your Father in heaven.' "

Relationship Builders

- Official Catholic doctrine says that good works have a place in salvation.
  Do we both agree on the understanding that the Catholic Church does not teach salvation through works but works resulting from salvation accepted through a genuine faith?

- Official Protestant doctrine does not link works with salvation, but Protestants do believe that a living faith will result in good works.
  Do we clearly understand how Protestants view good works?
  Do we agree upon the role of good works in the life of a Christian?

- Neither Catholics nor Protestants believe that works alone will earn salvation.
  Do we agree that a genuine faith in Jesus' saving redemption is what is needed for salvation, not works?

- Some Catholics may abuse the Catholic sacraments, giving the appearance that all Catholics use the sacraments as a means of earning salvation.

  Has either of us experienced a Catholic abusing a sacrament, affecting our view of Catholics as a whole?

  Have our perceptions negatively impacted our interfaith relationship?

BELIEF 8

We Believe in the Existence of Satan and Hell

*[B]e strong in the Lord and in the strength of his power. . . .
For our struggle is not against enemies of blood and flesh, but
against the rulers, against the authorities, against the cosmic
powers of this present darkness, against the spiritual forces of
evil in the heavenly places* (Ephesians 6:10, 12).

On a trip to Florida, Brian and I met with his college friend, a
Christian holistic doctor of Asian medicine. He took us onto a
beach one night to try to teach us to see auras, the energy that is said to
surround every living thing. What Brian and I both saw—independently,
as we were standing about 150 feet apart—appeared to be spirits,
figures of shadows and light. Brian especially was able to see these
figures and continued to see them around us even after we returned
home. Although we'd like to believe that these figures are angels, we
can't know that for sure because Paul tells us that "even Satan disguises
himself as an angel of light" (2 Corinthians 11:14). Seeing these figures
firsthand has brought into our realm of experience the reality of
spirits—both good and bad—and the possibility that they can literally
surround us continuously. And it is the negative influence of those
spirits that are evil that we as Christians must learn to recognize
and resist with the help of Jesus Christ. "Submit yourselves therefore

to God," James says. "Resist the devil, and he will flee from you" (James 4:7).

Before we can recognize the evil influences in our lives, however, we must understand the nature from which the influences come. Satan is a fallen angel who, along with other demons, was created naturally good by God but turned away from God out of envy: "[T]hrough the devil's envy death entered the world" (Wisdom of Solomon 2:24). Satan is a real entity, not just a symbolic biblical reference. Christian writer C. S. Lewis argues that "Satan's most effective strategy today in luring people to damnation is to make people believe that he doesn't exist, or exists only as a comical figure with horns and hoofs."[20]

Just as real as Satan is the existence of hell, the "state of definitive self-exclusion from communion with God and the blessed,"[21] "where their worm never dies, and the fire is never quenched" (Mark 9:48). Jesus tells us that "all causes of sin and all evildoers" will be thrown into this fire, where there will be "weeping and gnashing of teeth" (Matthew 13:41–42). Denying the existence of Satan or refusing to believe in hell is also refusing to take God seriously and, through that act, giving more power to Satan.

From Adam and Eve through this present day, a very real Satan— "the ruler of the power of the air, the spirit that is now at work among those who are disobedient" (Ephesians 2:2)—has attempted to cause people to sin and turn away from God through a variety of temptations. When one tactic doesn't work, he turns to another, much as he did to Jesus when tempting him for 40 days in the desert (Matthew 4:1–11; Luke 4:1–13). Scripture tells us that "when the devil had finished every test, he departed from him until an opportune time" (Luke 4:13). In the same way, Satan comes at us from different angles. When we use our faith to swat at him, as at a bee, he comes back again in a different spot, sometimes retreating for awhile to wait for a more "opportune time."

What forms can Satan's attacks take? Satan can use every doubt, misconception, and weakness to accomplish his purpose, which is to drive you and other Christians apart and away from God. As was stated

[20]C. S. Lewis, *The Screwtape Letters,* Letter VII (Old Tappan, N.J.: Fleming H. Revell, 1976), 45–46.
[21]*CCC,* 1033.

in this section's Introduction, a technique used by Satan in today's society to separate Christians is to cultivate the difference in beliefs between Catholics and Protestants. Satan will also use these differences to try to weaken or destroy your interfaith relationship. Being aware of the beliefs that unite you as Christians while recognizing that your differences are related to non-core beliefs is one way you can overcome Satan's obstacles to a united Christian relationship. (For more discussion about how Satan threatens Christian relationships and marriages, see page 199, *Discussion 1: How Do We Begin to Build a Unified, Faith-Based Relationship?*)

As Catholic and Protestant Christians, we must learn to resist Satan's influences by engaging in what some have referred to as spiritual warfare. In Ephesians, Paul tells us to prepare for the battle by "put[ting] on the whole armor of God, so that you may be able to stand against the wiles of the devil" (Ephesians 6:11):

> *Stand therefore, and fasten the belt of truth around your waist, and put on the breastplate of righteousness. As shoes for your feet put on whatever will make you ready to proclaim the gospel of peace. With all of these, take the shield of faith, with which you will be able to quench all the flaming arrows of the evil one. Take the helmet of salvation, and the sword of the Spirit, which is the word of God. Pray in the Spirit at all times in every prayer and supplication* (Ephesians 6:14–18).

The core Christian faith principles that Paul refers to in this passage—truth, righteousness, the gospel of peace, faith, salvation, the word of God, and prayer—are all discussed in the first section of this book and are some of the core beliefs that you and your partner need to focus on to build your Christian interfaith relationship. By putting on this "armor" of core Christian faith beliefs, you will be better able to resist the threats Satan will make to your interfaith relationship.

Anticipate that Satan will cause some strife in your life, and learn to properly control your reaction to it, and to God. In our married life together, Brian and I have gone through cyclical bouts of trials and tests.

At least some of these trials have likely been Satan testing us, with God's permission, as in the case of Job. Our reaction to these was consistently complaining to God that, essentially, we didn't deserve the trials we were going through. And the trials kept on coming. During one of these times, I was called to read through God's response to Job (Job 38–41), upon which I realized that we have no right to question God or what he allows to happen to us. We have no right to demand that the trials cease, but the Bible tells us that we can ask for God's mercy and strength and pray that, in his mercy, he will grant relief from the trials: "O Lord, you will hear the desire of the meek; you will strengthen their heart" (Psalm 10:17). When you face the inevitable trials and tribulations in your interfaith relationship, remember to maintain a humble attitude toward God and never waver in your trust of him: "Trust in the Lord forever, for in the Lord God you have an everlasting rock" (Isaiah 26:4). Remember that God has the power to use even Satan's evil intentions for good.

Relationship Builders

* Satan is a real "fallen angel," not a symbolic figure, in the same way that hell is real.
  Do we both agree that Satan is a real threat to us and to our interfaith relationship?
  If we don't acknowledge him as real, we inadvertently provide him with the guise of secrecy within which to negatively influence our lives.
  Do we also recognize that banishment to hell is a real consequence of sin?

* "The ruler of the power of the air" and his minions continuously tempt all people, including Christians.
  What are some of our weaknesses or doubts that Satan has used against us in the past?
  What is he using to cause conflicts between us right now?
  What are some tactics he could use against us in the future?

- The apostle Paul commands us to take up the "whole armor of God" in order to resist evil.

  What are some steps we can take to incorporate truth, righteousness, the gospel of peace, faith, salvation, the word of God, and prayer into our lives?

  What benefits could this have to our interfaith relationship?

- When faced with trials, Christians should maintain a humble attitude toward God.

  Has either of us reacted incorrectly to God when faced with hardships?

  How could we respond more appropriately to God as a unified couple when faced with trials in the future?

BELIEF 9

We Believe in the Reality of Sin and the Forgiveness of Sins

Then I acknowledged my sin to you, and I did not hide my iniquity; I said, "I will confess my transgressions to the LORD," and you forgave the guilt of my sin (Psalm 32:5).

One Sunday, Brian, our son Matthew, and I were having a very good day together, having had dinner with my parents and grandparents and enjoyed everyone's company. This day was a nice reprieve for us because, at that time, we were worried about several aspects of our lives that were unstable. During one of our conversations that day, we began discussing the unstable issues. With the optimism of the day buoying us up, we decided that our only recourse in coping with the instability was to fully trust God and not try to figure out for ourselves why certain things might be happening: "Trust in the LORD with all your heart, and do not rely on your own insight" (Proverbs 3:5). Strangely, the day seemed to turn at that point. Without even realizing it, we began to argue and bicker about some petty issue well into the evening. Not until we stopped fighting long enough to hear what we had actually been saying did we realize that we were in the grip of sin. This was an example of something that happens often in our relationship: Whenever we get close to understanding something related to our spiritual health and well-being—in this case, trusting God—our naturally sinful nature distracts us from what may ultimately bring us closer to God.

Understanding the nature of sin and the ways in which you might be susceptible to sin can help you resist this obstacle to an intimate relationship with each other and with God.

Just as Catholics and Protestants both believe in Satan, both believe in the existence of sin, which Paul defines as "everything that does not come from faith" (Romans 14:23). Sin was not something God intended for man. But as a result of Satan's jealousy and influence, sin and disobedience entered the world through Adam and Eve and continue to wreak havoc in all aspects of life, from the weeds in the garden, to the wars in the Middle East, to the conflicts in your interfaith relationship.

Because of Adam and Eve's original sin, all people are inherently sinful—"just as sin came into the world through one man, and death came through sin, and so death spread to all because all have sinned" (Romans 5:12). Even children aren't exempt from sin, which is why they tend to misbehave, author and actress Lisa Whelchel points out when describing her son, Tucker, in her parenting book, *Creative Correction*:

> *Tucker, like all of us, is a son of Adam, the first child on earth—so he comes by his sin naturally. In fact, the roots of misbehavior can be traced all the way back to Adam. Sin has less to do with our parenting ability and more to do with the state of our kids' hearts.*[22]

In the same way that Satan caused Adam and Eve to sin by disobeying God, he continues to prompt and prod people today to sin against God, taking advantage of some of the same sinful aspects of human nature that caused Adam and Eve to fall: pride, greed, and envy. These sins, along with anger, lust, gluttony, and laziness, are referred to

---

[22]Lisa Whelchel, *Creative Correction* (Wheaton, Ill.: Tyndale House Publishers, Inc., 2000), xiv.

by the *Catechism* as "capital" or "deadly" sins because they, in turn, cause other sins.[23]

Sin can take many different forms, such as those described by Paul in Galatians 5:19–21 ("fornication, impurity, licentiousness, idolatry, sorcery, enmities, strife, jealousy, anger, quarrels, dissensions, factions, envy, drunkenness, carousing, and things like these"). But sin is always an offense against God.

Even though Adam and Eve's fall made sin a permanent aspect of human nature, God maintained his love for mankind and desired to regain the intimate relationship with him that he had originally intended. Therefore God formed the Israelites, chosen people who would belong to God and learn to obey his will and through whom all humans would learn of the saving power of God. Out of these people, God brought forth his son, "born of a woman, born under the law" (Galatians 4:4), whose obedience satisfied God's justice and averted from mankind God's wrath instigated by sin. "For God has done what the law, weakened by the flesh, could not do: by sending his own Son in the likeness of sinful flesh, and to deal with sin, he condemned sin in the flesh, so that the just requirement of the law might be fulfilled in us, who walk not according to the flesh but according to the Spirit" (Romans 8:3–4). (The role of Jesus Christ in banishing sin and once again making salvation possible for all mankind is discussed more deeply beginning on page 31, *Belief 2: We Believe in Jesus Christ.*)

Jesus Christ sacrificed his life to pay the penalty for our sins, and, in doing so, he absorbed God's wrath for our sins. However, sins still have consequences, another point regarding sin about which Catholics and Protestants agree. We still suffer the consequences of Adam and Eve's original sin in the form of painful childbirth for women (Genesis 3:16) and the need for hard working of the land for food for men (Genesis 3:17–18). We also suffer with their sin's ultimate penalty, death, as God explained to Adam: " 'By the sweat of your face you shall eat bread until you return to the ground, for out of it you were taken; you are dust, and to dust you shall return' " (Genesis 3:19). And as sin

---

[23]CCC, 1866.

continued throughout the generations, so did the consequences of sin, such as in Deuteronomy 28:58–59 when Moses describes the penalty for disobedience:

> *If you do not diligently observe all the words of this law that are written in this book, fearing this glorious and awesome name, the LORD your God, then the LORD will overwhelm both you and your offspring with severe and lasting afflictions and grievous and lasting maladies.*

Not only are the people committing the sin paying the penalties for that sin, but the Bible also tells us that the consequences or penalties of the sin can be passed on to future generations, much as the penalties of Adam and Eve have been inherited. The book of Lamentations, which focuses on the penalties imposed upon Judah due to unrepentant sins, describes how sins have been passed on to future generations: "Our ancestors sinned; they are no more, and we bear their iniquities" (Lamentations 5:7). Graham, speaking about the high number of couples living together outside of marriage today, asks, "Can there be any question that the social diseases which now sweep our land as perhaps never before are an indication that man cannot flaunt the laws of God without paying some kind of penalty for his rebellion?"[24] Some Christian writers say that certain families with a history of specific addictions or medical problems may be suffering from the consequences of sins of their ancestors. Whether or not a sin like this may be affecting your interfaith relationship is something you need to pray about.

Because our God is a merciful God, he also promises to forgive the sins of those who are genuinely sorry for them, another belief that Catholics and Protestants hold in common. Even before the birth of Jesus, God promised forgiveness to his people, Israel, if only they would repent and turn from their sin. To Solomon, he said regarding Israel, " '[I]f my people who are called by my name humble themselves, pray, seek my face, and turn from their wicked ways, then I will hear from heaven, and will forgive their sin and heal their land' " (2 Chronicles.

---

[24]Graham, *Unto the Hills,* 119.

7:14). And in Acts 10:43, Peter attests, " 'All the prophets testify about him that everyone who believes in him receives forgiveness of sins through his name.' "

In addition to wanting us to be reconciled with him through confession and forgiveness of sins, God also wants Christians to be reconciled with each other. Therefore, Jesus says, " 'Whenever you stand praying, forgive, if you have anything against anyone; so that your Father in heaven may also forgive you your trespasses' " (Mark 11:25).

Be cognizant of the ways in which sin can manifest itself in your lives and in your interfaith relationship. Not only was Adam and Eve's sin, described in Genesis 3:1–6, the first sin, but it was also the "blueprint" for every sin committed since then. First, a person questions God. Next, the person is tempted to believe what he or she knows is not true. Third, a person's ego and pride is tapped. And finally, the person actually commits the sin. If you can spot the precursors to sin in your lives, you may be able to avoid the sins. But know that God is always willing to forgive if you do succumb to the unavoidable pressures of sin.

Relationship Builders

- Ever since the original sin of Adam and Eve, everyone has been subject to sin. However, Jesus Christ absorbed God's wrath for every sin that has been and would ever be committed.
  Through this ultimate sacrifice, God demonstrated his immense love for us, a love that continues to sustain us through our relationship difficulties. In what ways can we more fully rely on God's love within our interfaith relationship?

- Sin, even forgiven sin, has consequences.
  Could any of our relationship difficulties be a result of sins either of us has committed in the past?
  Does either of us have any unconfessed sins from the past that may be causing us problems today?
  Is it possible that some of our problems might be related to sins committed by our ancestors?

- God promises to forgive sins confessed with genuine sorrow and the sincere resolve to try to not repeat the sin.

    God's promise of forgiveness allows us to confess sins and be free of the guilt of sin. Is guilt from a former sin affecting our relationship in any way?

    Can we let go of this guilt, knowing that God has forgiven us?

- The circumstances leading up to Adam and Eve's sin provide us with an outline for every sin.

    How might knowing the precursors of sin make it easier for us to resist sin?

BELIEF 10

We Believe in the Importance of Baptism

Peter said to them, "Repent, and be baptized every one of you in the name of Jesus Christ so that your sins may be forgiven; and you will receive the gift of the Holy Spirit. For the promise is for you, for your children, and for all who are far away, everyone whom the Lord our God calls to him" (Acts 2:38–39).

B rian's dad is an ordained minister in a nondenominational Christian church. Since accepting this position, he has done some unusual duties, including baptizing new Christians in the local YMCA swimming pool. Both Brian and I were taken aback at the mental image of someone being immersed in baptism in the same pool where our son takes swimming lessons. We were used to infant baptisms, where the baby is in a ceremonial white dress in a traditional church, being baptized with water from a traditional baptismal font. But although this place of baptism was a bit unorthodox to us, we understood the importance of the baptismal ritual to becoming a member of the Christian body.

Although the actual rituals may vary between denominations, Catholics and Protestants do agree that it is necessary to be baptized as a rite of initiation into the body of Christ. The sign of baptism is the bond that links together the entire body of Christians, including Catholics and Protestants. Paul tells us in 1 Corinthians 12:13, "For in the one Spirit we were all baptized into one body—Jews or Greeks, slaves or free—and we were all made to drink of one Spirit." The *Catechism* acknowledges this unity between Protestants and Catholics: "Baptism constitutes the foundation of communion among all Christians . . . 'Justified by faith in Baptism, [they] are incorporated into Christ; they therefore have a right to be called Christians, and with good reason are accepted as brothers by the children of the Catholic Church.' "[25]

Because Ephesians 4:5 refers to "one baptism" and because baptism permanently marks a person for Christ, Catholics accept all Christian baptisms as valid and don't practice rebaptism. Some Protestant churches and denominations will practice rebaptism if a person who was baptized as an infant desires to be rebaptized as a saved adult. And, although clergy are normally the administrators of baptism in both Catholic and Protestant churches, in a case of necessity, anyone can baptize with the intention "to will to do what the Church does when she baptizes, and to apply the Trinitarian baptismal formula."[26]

Water is the common element used in baptism because water symbolizes refreshment and life, along with death by water. Baptism is prefigured in several incidents involving water in the Old Testament. Mankind was purged of sin through the waters of the Great Flood, where Noah and his family were saved through water but the remaining, sinful people all perished (see Genesis 7–9 and 1 Peter 3:20). The Israelites were also saved through crossing the waters of the Red Sea, where the same waters resulted in death for the Egyptians (see Exodus 14). Some biblical scholars even argue that Jonah was cleansed from his sin of disobeying God through the three days he spent in the fish in the water (see Jonah 1:17).

But water is only the earthly dimension of baptism. Through baptism, some Christians believe that the recipient also receives the gift of the Holy Spirit, initially given to the apostles at Pentecost

---

[25]*CCC*, 1271, partially quoting *Unitatis redintegratio*, 3.
[26]*CCC*, 1256.

(Acts 2:1–4), reflecting how the Spirit descended on Christ following his baptism (Matthew 3:16). Jesus' baptism was also symbolic of the baptism through suffering that was ahead of him, as he describes in Luke 12:50: " 'I have a baptism with which to be baptized, and what stress I am under until it is completed!' " Our baptism reflects Christ's baptism by water and the Spirit, along with his baptism by suffering, and allows us to share in the newness of life bought by his suffering, death, and resurrection. "Therefore we have been buried with him by baptism into death, so that, just as Christ was raised from the dead by the glory of the Father, so we too might walk in newness of life" (Romans 6:4).

Catholics and Protestants both refer to baptism as a "sacrament" because they agree that it is a religious practice that was instituted or recognized by Christ. Catholics assert that baptism is necessary for salvation, based on what Jesus said to Nicodemus in John 3:5: " 'Very truly I tell you, no one can enter the kingdom of God without being born of water and Spirit.' " When questioned how one should be saved, Peter reiterates Jesus' command in Acts 2:38 (cited on page 71). As in the case of good works, Protestants don't link baptism with salvation in official doctrine, but they still believe as Catholics do that Christians should be baptized as initiation into the body of Christ. And both Catholics and Protestants agree that a person is saved not through the baptismal ritual itself, but through the faith that prompts the person to want to receive baptism and live the life of a Christian.

Although Catholics and Protestants agree in the importance of baptism, Christians—including those of Protestant denominations—disagree as to whether a person should be baptized as an infant or as an adult. The Bible doesn't provide clear guidelines as to whether or not infants should be baptized, and proponents of both infant baptism and adult baptism have found Scripture to support their positions.

The Catholic Church and some Protestant denominations have traditionally chosen to practice infant baptism. Infant baptism is viewed as the sign of the new covenant much as circumcision, done when a male was eight days old, was the sign of the old covenant, as indicated in Colossians 2:11–12. Furthermore, in the covenant God established with Noah in Genesis 9:8–17 and with Abraham in Genesis 17:10–14, their children were included. Children were also welcomed by Jesus in the New Testament, such as in Mark 10:14 when Jesus says, " 'Let the little children come to me; do not stop them; for it is to such as these that the kingdom of God belongs.' " Also, passages such as Acts 2:39 ("the promise is for you, for your children, and for all who are far away") seem to indicate that baptism is intended for whole families, including children.

Because baptism is a sign of salvation, Protestants who favor adult baptism believe that a person can't receive this sign of salvation until he or she has the mature faith that is necessary for justification and salvation and can personally accept the gift of salvation from Christ. Children, especially infants, don't have a mature faith and aren't capable of making this crucial decision; therefore, some Protestants believe that they shouldn't be baptized. Some Protestants also argue that the Bible does not teach that one person can have faith for another, including a parent having faith for a child. In addition, some Protestants also say that Mark 10:14, where Jesus blesses the children, doesn't support infant baptism because no water is involved in the blessing.

Protestant denominations that do practice adult baptism, however, often have a dedication ceremony for the infant. This ceremony is much like an infant baptism, minus the water. In a dedication ceremony, the infant is dedicated to Christ and welcomed into the body of Christ, the church.

Another aspect of debate regarding baptism is its nature. Catholics view baptism as actually conferring grace and salvation, while Protestants typically see baptism as more of a symbolic, outward sign of one's inner salvation. Likewise, while Catholics view baptism as a sacrament of regeneration, Protestants view it more as a testimony to regeneration.

Catholics believe that in baptism, the Holy Spirit literally descends upon the individual and imparts the grace of God, regenerating, justifying, and saving the individual, along with beginning the process of sanctification. Faith in Christ is necessary for a newly converted adult to be baptized, but children can be justified and saved through the faith of their parents. In support of this belief, Catholics cite examples in the Bible such as Mark 5:22–23 and 35–43 and Mark 9:17–27 where the children were saved not by their own faith but through the faith of their parents. But baptism only plants a seed of faith that must be cultivated by the parents and the child as he or she grows: "The Catholic Church also teaches that the parents of the baptized child must commit themselves to providing an environment for the child to grow in faith. This will prepare the child to make a personal faith commitment to Jesus Christ upon reaching maturity. This personal faith commitment is absolutely necessary for the mature Christian."[27] Catholics believe that baptism has three effects on a person: a person's sins are forgiven and he or she receives God's grace; a person receives the Holy Spirit; and the person becomes a member of the body of Christ.

Protestants have varying views on baptism. Rather than conferring grace, Protestants typically view baptism as an outward sign of the grace through faith that is already present or that will be present when a person accepts Christ and is saved. Protestants also believe that faith is necessary for infant baptism. Some believe, like Catholics, that infants are baptized through the faith of their parents, who promise to raise the child in faith until he or she can make a mature commitment to Christ. Other Protestants believe that baptism is a sign of future faith, which will lead to salvation. And still other Protestants believe similarly to Catholics—and to Protestants like Martin Luther—that, because faith is a free gift from God, infants can actually receive saving faith through baptism.

Although some Protestants do believe similarly to Catholics that God uses baptism to dispense grace and salvation and as a means to literally send his Holy Spirit into a person, Protestants typically don't view baptism as taking away sin or imparting salvation. Rather, children will be saved when they grow mature and are able to make a conscious commitment to Christ. Some Protestants who practice adult baptism

---

[27]Schreck, *Catholic and Christian*, 128.

believe the person needs to have first accepted Christ and received salvation; thus, baptism becomes an outward sign of that person's internal salvation and membership in the body of Christ. Other Protestants believe that adults who have accepted Christ aren't saved until they are baptized.[28]

Another point of difference between Christians is the method by which baptism is administered: immersion, pouring, or sprinkling. Each method emphasizes a particular benefit of baptism. Immersion identifies a person with the death, burial, and resurrection of Christ; pouring signifies the outpouring of the Holy Spirit; and sprinkling symbolizes the cleansing of sins by Christ's blood. The Catholic Church typically baptizes infants using the pouring method. Protestants churches vary in their use of immersion, pouring, and sprinkling.

Despite their differences, Catholics and Protestants agree that with baptism comes certain responsibilities. Because a baptized person belongs to God, he or she must live a life of Christ. The person needs to possess a faith that is active in Christian charity, contributing to personal and universal sanctification. This obligation as a Christian includes obeying Christ's Great Commission to spread his gospel throughout the world.

You can use your baptism as a point of unity in your interfaith relationship. Look for elements about baptism with which you agree and move on from there to discuss why you may disagree with others. Articulating your common beliefs about baptism now will also help when you have to decide how and when to baptize your children. (See also page 229, *Discussion 6: In What Religion Will We Raise Our Children?*).

Relationship Builders

• Baptism is the bond that links together the whole body of Christ.
 In spite of our denominational differences, we are united as
  Christians through the bond of baptism. Have we consciously

---

[28]Erwin Lutzer, *The Doctrines That Divide: A Fresh Look at the Historic Doctrines That Separate Christians,* 2d ed. (Grand Rapids, Mich.: Kregel Publications, 1998), 134.

*looked beyond our differences to acknowledge this bond of unity
we have together in Christ?*

*In what ways could we build upon our unity of baptism to strengthen
our interfaith relationship?*

- The elements of baptism are water and, some Christians believe, the
Holy Spirit.

   *Which of these elements do we accept as being a part of the
   baptismal ritual?*

   *Can we find unity within our beliefs? If not, on what points do we
   disagree? Why?*

- Catholics believe in baptizing infants, whereupon the Holy Spirit
descends upon the infant, regenerating, justifying, and saving the
child.

   *For the Catholic: Are these my beliefs regarding baptism?
   Why or why not?*

   *For the Protestant: With which of these beliefs do I agree and
   disagree?*

- Protestants vary in their views of baptism. Some believe in infant
baptism, while some support adult baptism, with infants being
dedicated to Christ. And generally, Protestants see baptism as an
outward, symbolic sign of one's future or inner salvation.

   For the Protestant: What do I personally believe about baptism?

   *For the Catholic: With which of my partner's beliefs do I agree and
   disagree?*

BELIEF 11

We Believe in the Need to Pray and the Power of Prayer

And this is the boldness we have in him, that if we ask anything according to his will, he hears us. And if we know that he hears us in whatever we ask, we know that we have obtained the requests made of him (1 John 5:14–15).

From a young age, Catholics and Protestants are taught to pray to God, from the formal Catholic prayers that I was taught in catechism classes to the traditional bedtime prayers that my husband remembers learning from his parents. And although Catholic and Protestant prayers may take different forms—Catholics traditionally use a repertoire of formal prayers while Protestants generally are more spontaneous in their praying—both denominations use prayer as a means of communicating with God, letting him know their needs, praising him for blessings, and asking him for forgiveness.

In fact, Brian and I believe that our prayers actually resulted in our relationship. Around the same time, we concluded later, Brian (in Florida) and I (in Pennsylvania) were both moved by the Holy Spirit to go to our pastor and priest respectively and express our desire to meet that right person. Both of us were lonely and strongly wanted to settle down with someone. Pastor and priest alike advised us to pray that our need for lifetime companionship would be fulfilled. We did, and within a month we had found each other.

Our relationship is an example of how God does answer our prayers when they are in line with his will. The Holy Spirit also prompted us to seek out religious leaders who could guide us in our prayers because "we do not know how to pray as we ought, but that very Spirit intercedes with sighs too deep for words" (Romans 8:26).

One mistake we sometimes make in prayer, however, is merely reciting words and not truly having faith that God will hear us and answer our prayer. The *Catechism* calls this faith "filial boldness,"[29] and it is reflected in Jesus' words in Mark 11:24: " 'So I tell you, whatever you ask for in prayer, believe that you have received it, and it will be yours.' " And in Matthew 9:13, Jesus rebuked the Pharisees for their adherence to the ritualistic elements of religion, including reciting prayers, without inner faith. Jesus was condemning prayers that were merely recited, not repetitious prayers said with true faith, repetitious praying being a practice for which Catholics are sometimes criticized.

Brian and I learned most poignantly just how necessary faith is to prayer after the birth of our son, Matthew.

After Matthew was born, I left a well-paying corporate job to stay at home full time, a decision that Brian and I both strongly felt was in line with God's will. Going from two incomes to one was a financial blow to our family. We depreciated our savings just living day-to-day and truly feared that the time would come when we literally ran out of money. We begged God for help, but no noticeable relief came.

In the midst of our strife, I stumbled across this passage from James 1:5–8:

> *If any of you is lacking in wisdom, ask God, who gives to all generously and ungrudgingly, and it will be given you. But ask in faith, never doubting, for the one who doubts is like a wave of the sea, driven and tossed by the wind; for the doubter, being double-minded and unstable in every way, must not expect to receive anything from the LORD.*

---

[29]*CCC,* 2610.

What this passage said to me was that even though we were praying for financial help, we both doubted inside that it would come because we, with our shortsighted vision, couldn't see how it would come. Our family was literally being "driven and tossed" by our financial instability. I shared my insight with Brian, and from that point on, we have genuinely tried to put our complete trust in God that he will hear our prayers and solve our problems. And he has, in almost miraculous ways that have exceeded our expectations.

The confidence and security in God's provisions with which we should approach prayer are reiterated throughout both the Old and New Testaments. Psalm 145:18 says, "The Lord is near to all who call on him, to all who call on him in truth." In Mark 11:24, Jesus says, " 'So I tell you, whatever you ask for in prayer, believe that you have received it, and it will be yours.' " And in Matthew 21:22, he says, " 'Whatever you ask for in prayer with faith, you will receive.' "

In addition to speaking, prayer should include quiet time to listen for God's answer, as God says in Psalm 46:10: " 'Be still, and know that I am God!' " I once attended a lecture given by an Indian priest who suggested that a prayer session include quiet preparation, biblical readings, and meditation before the spoken prayer and contemplation after the spoken prayer. By incorporating quiet times into your prayers, you invite God into your heart and mind to give you direction not only for your interfaith relationship but also for all other aspects of your life as well. When you stop long enough to listen to God, you will be amazed at all he wants to say to you directly!

One final thing that is important to remember about prayer is to just do it! Even though we know that prayer is important and that "the prayer of the righteous is powerful and effective" (James 5:16), we sometimes get so wrapped up in our problems that we forget to pray. God wants us to ask for help; he wants us to depend on him and look to him for answers. Sometimes we don't receive what we think we need simply because we have neglected to ask for it. Jesus himself tells us: " 'Ask, and it will be given you; search, and you will find; knock, and the door will be opened for you. For everyone who asks receives, and everyone who searches finds, and for everyone who knocks, the door will be opened' " (Matthew 7:7–8). Remember to pray.

Relationship Builders

- God will answer our prayers when they are in line with his will.
  Do we both genuinely believe that our interfaith relationship is part of the will of God?

- The Holy Spirit will intercede for us with God, guiding our prayers.
  Are we willing to ask for the Holy Spirit's guidance in praying for our relationship?
  Are we comfortable praying for this guidance together?

- We need to have unwavering faith that God will hear and answer our prayers.
  Do we inherently trust that God will hear our prayers and provide us with the understanding and wisdom needed to overcome the obstacles in our relationship?

- Some of our prayer time should be spent listening, not talking.
  Do we allow quiet time in our prayers to hear God's guidance for our lives and insight into our interfaith relationship?

BELIEF 12

We Believe in Fasting as a Way of Drawing Closer to God

Then the disciples of John came to [Jesus], saying, "Why do we and the Pharisees fast often, but your disciples do not fast?" And Jesus said to them, "The wedding guests cannot mourn as long as the bridegroom is with them, can they? The days will come when the bridegroom is taken away from them, and then they will fast" (Matthew 9:14–15).

As a Catholic growing up with a majority of Protestant friends, I faced seemingly endless questions in the school cafeteria about why I didn't eat meat on Fridays during Lent. I really didn't know how to respond to my friends; that's just what I was taught to do. I was also asked why Catholics give up candy and other things during Lent, another question I couldn't answer. That's just what Catholics did.

Maybe you as a Catholic were in similar situations, and you as a Protestant had similar questions as my friends. I've found that people of one denomination often question and sometimes discount practices that someone from another denomination can't explain in detail, such as the

Catholic fasting during Lent. Perhaps you have even experienced this type of conflict within your interfaith relationship. Despite their different viewpoints and approaches, however, both Catholics and Protestants practice fasting and believe that fasting is a way to draw closer to God and enhance one's relationship with God.

The Catholic Church has certain requirements that involve fasting, which may be why Catholics are more often associated with practicing fasting than Protestants. During Lent primarily, Catholics practice both abstaining from meat and fasting by limiting the amount of food intake. Catholics who have attained the age of fourteen are required to abstain from eating meat on Fridays during Lent and also on the first day of Lent, Ash Wednesday. Catholics are not required to eat fish on these days, just to abstain from meat because avoiding this diet staple is considered to be a sacrifice. Friday is chosen as the day of abstinence to remind people of Christ's sacrifice on Good Friday and the sacrifices that we should make in union with his.

In addition, Catholics who have reached the age of twenty-one are required to fast on Ash Wednesday and Good Friday, having only two small meals and one main meal, with no eating between meals. The age ranges for both abstaining from meat and fasting are designated to exclude the very young and the very old, who may have medical difficulties from participating.

Although not required by the Catholic Church, many Catholics voluntarily choose to give up something pleasurable during the season of Lent, such as eating candy, to also reflect Christ's sacrifice and draw closer to God during this time. Some may also choose to enhance their relationship with God and enrich their spiritual lives by beginning new practices during this time, such as daily Bible readings or exercise in conjunction with prayer.

Though Protestant fasting isn't as regimented or required, it is practiced and encouraged within most Protestant churches and denominations. Typically, Protestant fasting will involve going without food or eating only a minimal amount of food for a certain period of time, rather than only on designated days like the Catholic Lenten fasting.

The Bible includes many passages in both the Old and New Testaments that support fasting. In Isaiah 58:1–9, God describes how his people "delight to draw near to God" (Isaiah 58:2) but use self–centered fasting to try to do so. In this passage, God explains that the kind of fasting that will make the Lord hear their cries is the kind that helps to support the needs of their neighbors. In Joel 2:12, God asks his people to "return to me with all your heart, with fasting, with weeping, and with mourning." In Acts 13:2 and 14:23, disciples of the Lord are described as combining fasting with their prayers. And Jesus himself "fasted forty days and forty nights" (Matthew 4:2) in the wilderness before he began his public ministry. Jesus even provides guidelines for fasting in Matthew 6:16–18.

However they choose to practice fasting, Catholics and Protestants both have the same purposes in fasting: to draw closer to God and to enhance their relationship with him. Through deprivation, fasting mourns the death of Christ in his ultimate sacrifice and the temporary departure of him from this earth. In Matthew 9:14–15, cited earlier, Jesus explains how the disciples don't fast when they are with him because they don't need to draw closer to God at that time; God is already among them, and they don't need to mourn the loss of his presence. But when Jesus leaves, the disciples will need to fast for the purpose of drawing closer to him again. Although in the presence of the Holy Spirit, modern-day Christians are not fortunate enough to have been in the presence of the incarnate God as the disciples were, so we are in the position that they were after Jesus left, needing to fast in order to draw closer to Christ. Through eliminating the focus on earthly food, fasting helps Christians to more clearly focus on the spiritual God and perhaps more clearly hear his will for their lives.

Both Catholics and Protestants use fasting as a form of prayer in itself and also as an enhancement to prayer. Some believe that combining fasting with prayer can make their prayer requests more effective. In addition, through the deprivation of food, Christians are reminded of the blessings God provides in the form of these foods and in all other facets of life. The Catholic Church also considers fasting to be a form of penance, reparation (the act of making amends) for sins committed.

Neither Catholics nor Protestants believe that fasting will bring them salvation, for the Bible says explicitly that "the kingdom of God is not food and drink" (Romans 14:17). Nor is fasting required by Scripture: "Those who eat, eat in honor of the Lord, since they give thanks to God; while those who abstain, abstain in honor of the Lord and give thanks to God" (Romans 14:6). The Catholic Church makes its requirements for its members not because it is required by the Bible but because it firmly believes that through this fasting and abstinence from meat, its members can more fully serve and honor Christ and grow in spirituality and sanctification.

In our relationship, Brian and I both practice the Catholic Church's requirements for abstaining from meat and fasting during Lent. My reasoning for this is that I have learned and accepted why the Catholic Church requires Lenten abstinence and fasting, believing that the deprivation enhances my relationship with God and helps me to appreciate more deeply Christ's sacrifice.

"My primary reasoning for abstaining from meat and fasting during Lent is not because the Catholic Church requires it," says Brian, "but because I know that it is important to Sandy, and I don't want my actions, or nonparticipation in this case, to cause her to fail in her efforts. I try to abide by Romans 14:21, which says, 'It is good not to eat meat or drink wine or do anything that makes your brother or sister stumble.' "

Remember that Catholics and Protestants both support fasting and that you shouldn't judge each other just because your form of fasting may differ. "Those who eat must not despise those who abstain, and those who abstain must not pass judgment on those who eat; for God has welcomed them" (Romans 14:3).

Relationship Builders

• Although both groups practice fasting, Catholics and Protestants may differ in the specifics of how they fast, including what food or foods they are eliminating, the amount of food—if any—that they eat, the duration of the fast, and the time of year of the fast.
Has either of us ever fasted?
What elements did our fast include? What were our specific reasons for fasting?

• Evidence for fasting appears in both the Old and New Testaments.
What can we learn about sacrifice from these biblical references to fasting?
How could these insights be applied to our interfaith relationship?

• Christian purposes for fasting include drawing closer to God and enhancing our relationship with him. Christians also fast as a form of prayer, as a reminder of blessings, and even as a penance.
Would we consider fasting for the sake of our relationship?
What would our goals be for that type of fast?
What elements do we think that type of fast should include?

• Christians should support each other in fasting.
Do we encourage each other in our fasting?
In what ways could we be more supportive of each other's efforts?
What benefits could we realize by fasting together?

BELIEF 13

We Believe in Evangelization

Now the eleven disciples went to Galilee, to the mountain to which Jesus had directed them. When they saw him, they worshipped him; but some doubted. And Jesus came and said to them, "All authority in heaven and on earth has been given to me. Go therefore and make disciples of all nations, baptizing them in the name of the Father and of the Son and of the Holy Spirit, and teaching them to obey everything that I have commanded you. And remember, I am with you always, to the end of the age" (Matthew 28:16–20).

During his time on earth, Jesus taught his disciples many spiritual truths related to the salvation of all people. Just as Jesus says, " 'No one after lighting a lamp puts it under the bushel basket' " (Matthew 5:15), Jesus doesn't want his truths to be hidden. Therefore, his Spirit has blessed each Christian with one or more spiritual gifts, "the manifestation of the Spirit for the common good" (1 Corinthians 12:7). (See also 1 Corinthians 12:8–11, and *Belief 3: We Believe in the Holy Spirit* on page 37.) Each Christian is expected to use his or her God-given gifts to further the kingdom of God. Catholics and Protestants both take this call to evangelization seriously.

The primary purpose of evangelization is to spread the truths of the gospel, to convert nonbelievers to a belief in salvation through Christ. Conversion is turning away from that which opposes God and embracing the saving work of God through Christ and the Holy Spirit. The evangelization efforts of the church were first evident after Jesus appeared to the disciples following his resurrection. At this first meeting of the early Christian church, Thomas was absent. Later, the other disciples tried to convince Thomas of the real presence of Christ, saying, " 'We have seen the Lord' " (John 20:25). To this day, the goal of the Christian church is to convince non-believers that the Lord is alive, just as the disciples in that first church were trying to convince Thomas. However, Thomas didn't believe until he saw the Lord with his own eyes, but Jesus says of all those who convert, " 'Blessed are those who have not seen and yet have come to believe' " (John 20:29).

Some Christians may feel called to use their spiritual gifts to directly preach the gospel as a pastor, priest, other religious person, or missionary. Others may feel led to share the gospel through participation in church programs or outreach efforts. But even if we don't feel spiritually led to preach the gospel directly, we are still called to evangelize through our actions and works. As Sister Altemose poignantly says, "You may be the only Bible someone ever reads."[30] You want your words and actions to speak volumes about Christ, demonstrating God's love toward others and making them want to learn more about the God who can give this kind of love and provision for their needs. "Everything is for your sake," Paul says to the Corinthians, "so that grace, as it extends to more and more people, may increase thanksgiving, to the glory of God" (2 Corinthians 4:15).

Because of the differences in beliefs between Catholics and Protestants, often members of both of these denominations see part of their evangelization duty as trying to "win over" members of another denomination. This practice has been referred to as "proselytizing" or "sheep stealing" and has been condemned by the "Evangelicals and Catholics Together" statement when it takes the form of "recruiting people from another community for purposes of denominational or institutional aggrandizement." While defending proselytizing as a religious freedom, the statement also asks Christians to refrain from this

---

[30]Altemose, *Why Do Catholics . . . ?*, 163.

activity within the Christian body, acknowledging that discipleship growth opportunities are available in both Catholic and Protestant churches and that the religious allegiance of a committed Christian should be respected. The statement also points out that, because so many people throughout the world don't know the gospel, using efforts to try to "convert" other Christians is neither "theologically legitimate" nor a wise use of time and other resources.[31]

Proselytizing as described above is discouraged for targeting Christians who are active in and committed to a particular denomination. The same guideline applies to your interfaith relationship. If you are both committed Christians, even if one is Catholic and one is Protestant, you shouldn't try to convert one another. With the help of this book, you should use the spiritual gifts that God has given you to build upon your common Christian beliefs and establish a unified Christian relationship.

Evangelization efforts may be useful, however, in welcoming back a Christian who may have drifted from the practice of the Christian faith. For example, a nondenominational Protestant church may try to attract former Catholics who have stopped attending church altogether. In this case, people from one denomination are inviting other people to their church who are nonpracticing Catholics; the denomination is not trying to convert Catholics who are active in their church. In your relationship, if one of you isn't a Christian or maybe doesn't have a very strong faith or perhaps has drifted away from the faith, the other could use evangelization efforts to bring that person closer to Christ. But you should be very cautious when getting involved with someone at a different level of spiritual development than you. (For more guidance, see *Discussion 2: Are We Unequally Yoked?* on page 205.)

Evangelization not only benefits nonbelievers by enlightening them about Christ, it also benefits the Christian who teaches another about Christ either through word or action. By trying to live a faith-filled life that can encourage others to convert to Christ, the Christian draws closer to Christ and grows in sanctification, becoming more Christlike.

---

[31]Colson et al., "Evangelicals and Catholics Together."

One point that is assumed in this chapter but should be reiterated nonetheless is that, before you bring other people to Christ through evangelization, you yourself must become a disciple of Christ, a follower of him even if it means renouncing preferences and other personal things that might be important to you. Jesus himself requires us to do this in Mark 8:34–35 when he says, " 'If any want to become my followers, let them deny themselves and take up their cross and follow me. For those who want to save their life will lose it, and those who lose their life for my sake, and for the sake of the gospel, will save it.' " And all Christians want to be followers of Christ, for, as Peter says to Christ, " 'Lord, to whom can we go? You have the words of eternal life' " (John 6:68).

Relationship Builders

- Evangelization is converting nonbelievers to Christ.
  Have we been active evangelists? Why or why not?
  Has our interfaith relationship been a form of evangelism for each other?

- Every Christian has been given at least one spiritual gift for spreading the gospel through evangelization.
  What spiritual gifts have we identified within ourselves?
  In what ways have we tried to use these gifts in spreading the gospel message?
  How could we more effectively use the gifts that God has given us?

- Christians are discouraged from proselytizing as a form of evangelization.
  Has either of us tried to pressure the other to change religious denominations?
  What kind of strain has this effort placed on our relationship?
  Have we experienced any proselytizing outside of our relationship?
  How do we feel about this type of Christian-to-Christian religious pressure?

- Evangelization can also help Christians to grow in sanctification. *What personal benefits have we experienced from evangelization? If we haven't actively evangelized, in what ways could spreading the gospel help us become more Christlike?*

BELIEF 14

We Believe in the Truth of the Bible and the Importance of Bible Reading

All scripture is inspired by God and is useful for teaching, for reproof, for correction, and for training in righteousness, so that everyone who belongs to God may be proficient, equipped for every good work (2 Timothy 3:16–17).

When I hold a Bible in my hands, I am amazed to think that the answers to all of the world's problems, not to mention my personal concerns, are contained in there. The answers may not be crystal clear, but they are there. Knowing this, I shouldn't have been surprised when Brian's college friend, the doctor of holistic Asian medicine, told me that I was searching for life's answers in all the wrong places. I wasn't spending nearly enough time reading and studying the Word, and this lack of devotion reflected itself throughout my whole being.

As a young Catholic, however, I wasn't encouraged to read the Bible. Although access to the Bible isn't forbidden for Catholics, as some Protestants believe, in my religious education, emphasis was placed upon learning about the Catholic sacraments, prayers, and generally how to be a good person. The reading of Bible passages was most often reserved for church.

Brian, on the other hand, was raised completely on Scripture in the Protestant tradition, so he grew up with a solid foundational knowledge of the Bible. When we met, he was much better versed in the Bible than I was. It was through discussions with him that my zeal for studying the Scriptures was really ignited.

You may have a similar situation in your interfaith relationship, where one person is more intimate with the Scriptures than the other. Take advantage of this opportunity to teach each other and learn from each other about "the living and active" (Hebrews 4:12) Word of God. Second to prayer, studying the Word is the most important way to receive God's guidance for your interfaith relationship. In fact, God promises to help those who read and live by his Word: " 'If you abide in me, and my words abide in you, ask for whatever you wish, and it will be done for you' " (John 15:7). Let the Scripture be "a lamp to [your] feet and a light to [your] path" (Psalm 119:105) in your interfaith journey together.

Guidance for your relationship and other aspects of your lives may be provided in the actual content of the Bible passages you read. As you encounter various situations, relevant Bible passages may leap to mind, their content providing the necessary momentary insight. But reading the Bible can also help you better understand God's thought process, making you more capable of interpreting situations and making decisions that are in line with his will. "Meditating upon the Scriptures will saturate your mind with His mind," says Baptist pastor Dr. Charles Stanley, "helping you filter your circumstances through His wisdom."[32]

My husband's cousin provides an interesting perspective on another reason why Bible reading is so important. Eric believes that everyone has a personal ministry, and reading the Bible helps to refill those "waters" that flow out through ministering. Without supplementation from the Bible, one will stagnate like the Dead Sea, one of the saltiest

---

[32]Charles Stanley, *Enter His Gates* (Nashville: Thomas Nelson Publishers, 1998), 55.

bodies of water in the world. So stagnant and salty, in fact, that it sustains no life.

How can you integrate the Word more into your life? You can start by committing to reading some biblical passages each day, even just a line. You can read these passages together or independently, whichever works better for your methods of study. But it would be helpful to share any insights you receive with your partner. Because you are building a relationship together, you must also bring together your ideas. God may promote this sharing of ideas by giving one of you the specific insights and answers that the other is seeking.

You may also benefit from setting up a more formal reading schedule. Some people set aside a designated time each day in which they pray and read Scripture, writing down prayers, ideas, concerns, meaningful Bible passages, and other insights. Bible studies are another option available to you. Most Protestant churches offer Bible studies, and many Catholic churches are starting them as well. A Bible study will give you the opportunity to learn about Scripture in a group setting, receiving—and giving—unique perspectives and opinions.

In an attempt to become more intimate with the Word, however, be careful not to lose your focus on God, becoming so intent on the act of reading Scripture that you neglect to understand, accept, and follow the precepts about which you are reading. Jesus himself warns, " 'You search the scriptures because you think that in them you have eternal life; and it is they that testify on my behalf. Yet you refuse to come to me to have life' " (John 5:39). Be sure to use prayer to keep God in the forefront of all you do.

Relationship Builders

- Reading the Bible is one of the most important things you can do to receive guidance for your interfaith relationship.
  Do we each currently read the Bible on a regular basis? If not, would we be willing to start?

Are we also willing to let God into our relationship by sharing with each other the insights we receive through Bible reading?

- Reading the Bible is useful both for its content and for the perspective we gain into God's thought processes.
  How could reading Bible passages from these different perspectives provide different forms of guidance for our interfaith relationship?

- You can incorporate Scripture into your lives through formal and informal reading programs and Protestant or Catholic Bible studies.
  What type of a personal reading schedule would work best for each of us?
  Are we willing to attend a Protestant or Catholic Bible study together? Why or why not?

- In spite of its importance, the Bible is from God, not God itself.
  Do we promise to consciously hold God himself above all else, including the Bible, acknowledging the Bible as his creation, much as we are?

BELIEF 15

We Believe in Respecting the Sabbath

If you refrain from trampling the sabbath, from pursuing your own interests on my holy day; if you call the sabbath a delight and the holy day of the LORD honorable; if you honor it, not going your own ways, serving your own interests, or pursuing your own affairs; then you shall take delight in the LORD, and I will make you ride upon the heights of the earth; I will feed you with the heritage of your ancestor Jacob, for the mouth of the LORD has spoken (Isaiah 58:13–14).

S etting aside one day a week for God is a practice of both Catholics and Protestants that has its roots in the commandment that God gave to Moses on Mount Sinai (Exodus 20:8–11). The traditional Jewish Sabbath, which literally means "a time to rest," is on Saturday, the seventh day of the week. For Christians, the ceremonial observance of the Sabbath is on Sunday, the day that Jesus rose from the dead (Matthew 28:1).

Catholics and Protestants both believe in observing the Sabbath by normally attending church and not working on Sunday. Brian's grandmother would avoid doing any work on Sunday by many times making soup or roast on Saturday so it only had to be heated for dinner on

Sunday. Then after dinner, his grandparents would rinse and stack dishes in the sink to be washed on Monday. A priest at a church I once attended also emphasized that no work should be done on Sundays except cooking because that enabled a family to have important fellowship time together. In addition, this priest advised against shopping on Sundays because the patronage encourages stores to remain open on Sundays, forcing their employees to work.

Jesus and his disciples were criticized by some Pharisees for failing to observe the Sabbath, such as in Mark 2:23–24, when the disciples picked grain on the Sabbath, and in John 9:1–16, when Jesus healed the blind man on the Sabbath. To these criticisms, Jesus replied, " 'The sabbath was made for humankind, and not humankind for the sabbath; so the Son of Man is lord even of the Sabbath' " (Mark 2:27–28).

MacArthur might say that Jesus responded this way to criticisms because he knew that he had come to establish the new covenant, abolishing the old covenant with its related laws, including the Ten Commandments.[33] Most of the Ten Commandments have been restated and therefore revalidated in the New Testament, however, with the exception of the commandment regarding the sabbath. MacArthur says that Colossians 2:16 nullifies this commandment: "Therefore, do not let anyone condemn you in matters of food and drink or of observing festivals, new moons, or sabbaths."[34]

In Mark 2:27–28, Jesus may also have been saying that God provided the Sabbath for us as a time of necessary rest. God himself felt the need to take a day of rest after creation: "And on the seventh day God finished the work that he had done, and he rested on the seventh day from all the work that he had done" (Genesis 2:2). If God needed to rest, how can we, mere humans, even think we don't need to rest, or have too much to do to rest? And some people use that same excuse for not attending weekly worship services. A high school classmate once told me that he couldn't attend church on Sundays during the summer because he was too busy with his softball league. I questioned his priorities. For while attending church gives God the worship, praise, and

---

[33]MacArthur, *Study Bible,* 125.
[34]Ibid.

honor he deserves, it concurrently reminds us of our dependency on him. Lifting our hearts to him also opens our hearts to his grace and enriches us with his Spirit which, combined with the rest our bodies receive on Sundays, makes us that much more effective during the other six days of the week.

Brian and I have always been ones who knew we should observe the Sabbath but really did it halfheartedly. Yes, we did attend church each week. But when we returned from church, we would mow or do laundry or a myriad of other small tasks, not exactly heavy labor but work nonetheless. While we continued this practice, we noticed other areas of our life that were out of balance, mainly our financial situation. We had a modest amount of income, yet weren't able to save much or give much to the church. Brian was raised to give 10 percent of his income, his tithe, to the church. Yet our financial responsibilities made it virtually impossible to give 10 percent. Was there a connection between the way we observed the Sabbath, our lack of tithing, and our financial problems?

Yes! Just as Jesus opened the minds of the disciples following his resurrection ("Then he opened their minds to understand the scriptures," Luke 24:45), his Spirit opened our minds to the biblical links. Tithing isn't required in the New Testament; in 2 Corinthians 9:7, Paul says, "Each of you must give as you have made up your mind, not reluctantly or under compulsion, for God loves a cheerful giver." But like the observation of the Sabbath, most Christians adhere to this Old Testament law as a way to honor God and support his church. And Christians don't want to rob God of what is rightfully his, as is described in Malachi 3:8–9:

> *Will anyone rob God? Yet you are robbing me! But you say, "How are we robbing you?" In your tithes and offerings! You are cursed with a curse, for you are robbing me—the whole nation of you!*

Not only were Brian and I robbing God of our money, which was his, but we were also robbing him of our time, which was his also, as is everything. Jesus said, " 'Give therefore to the emperor the things that are the emperor's, and to God the things that are God's' " (Matthew 22:21), but we were doing neither. Therefore, we promised God that we would give as much as we could at the time, using what was needed to repay our debts, until the time came when we could fully tithe. In the meantime, we tried to compensate for our lack of donation of money with a rededication and donation of time of rest on the sabbath. Through our actions, we repeat the essence of Azariah's words in the furnace as inscribed in Daniel 3:38–41:

> In our day we have . . . no burnt offering, or sacrifice, or oblation, or incense, no place to make an offering before you and to find mercy. Yet with a contrite heart and a humble spirit may we be accepted, as though it were with burnt offerings of rams and bulls, or with tens of thousands of fat lambs; such may our sacrifice be in your sight today, and may we unreservedly follow you, for no shame will come to those who trust in you. And now with all our heart we follow you; we fear you and seek your presence.

You also need to evaluate what the Sabbath means to you and how you can best observe it together. It could be a time for you to learn more about each other, about your families, and about the different ways that you worship. Be sure not to squander the time that God has provided for your rejuvenation and renewal. Treat the time as the gift of reprieve that it is.

Relationship Builders

- Although not required by the New Testament, observing the Sabbath is still practiced by most Catholics and Protestants through refraining from work and attending church.
  Do we currently keep the Sabbath day holy? How?
  Do we believe that observing the Sabbath is something that we are called to do as Christians?

- God may have established the Sabbath as much a day of honor for him as a day of rest for humans.

  Do we take advantage of the opportunities for rest and rejuvenation on the Sabbath?

  Or do we feel that we have so much to do that we can't afford to rest?

  How might our lack of commitment to the Sabbath manifest itself in problems in our interfaith relationship?

- Respecting the Sabbath and tithing might be connected for some people.

  What is our attitude about tithing?

  Do we feel, like many others, that we don't have enough money to give 10 percent to the church for God's work?

  How might the problems within our relationship be related to our lack of tithing?

- Observing the Sabbath provides growth opportunities.

  What are some activities that we could do in conjunction with honoring the Sabbath that would enrich our interfaith relationship?

Part Two

ADDRESSING THE
DIFFERENCES IN
OUR BELIEFS

INTRODUCTION

The Reality of Differences

[B]rothers and sisters, I could not speak to you as spiritual people, but rather as people of the flesh, as infants in Christ. I fed you with milk, not solid food, for you were not ready for solid food. Even now you are still not ready, for you are still of the flesh. For as long as there is jealousy and quarreling among you, are you not of the flesh, and behaving according to human inclinations? For when one says, "I belong to Paul," and another, "I belong to Apollos," are you not merely human? (1 Corinthians 3:1–4)

Since the Protestant Reformation began in the sixteenth century as a reaction to those Roman Catholic doctrines and practices thought to be errant or corrupt, the divisions between Catholics and Protestants have continued to grow. Misunderstandings can contribute to these divisions, as well as simple prejudices. However, legitimate theological disagreements remain as the primary source of the conflicts between Catholics and Protestants, and these issues of genuine conflict are the focus of this second section of *United in Heart, Divided in Faith*.

Catholics and Protestants alike maintain that their respective belief systems and practices are wholly correct, perpetuating these divisions. The Catholic Church does recognize that the gospel message is taught in Protestant churches but holds that the richest practice of the faith is found within the Catholic Church because of its unbroken apostolic lineage.

Catholics believe that only Catholic church leaders are direct apostolic successors and are the only clergy ordained through the sacrament of Holy Orders, the sacrament which empowers priests to perform the other sacraments, including the sacrament of Holy Communion.

Protestants, on the other hand, hold that the Catholic Church has errantly added beliefs to the biblical message, teachings that detract from or compromise the message of the gospel. In explaining the Protestant perspective, author Karl Keating cites Rev. D. Martyn Lloyd-Jones as saying that the problem with Catholicism " 'is not so much a matter of "denial" of the truth, but rather such an addition to the truth that eventually it becomes a departure from it.' "[35]

Knowing that these differences in beliefs exist, you must approach discussing the issues that divide Catholics and Protestants with open minds and the desire to thoroughly understand each issue from both Catholic and Protestant perspectives. Altemose advises that when two people are in such a dialogue, each must first move the "fences" blocking their communication and understanding, including:

1. The fence of exclusiveness, where one's ideas are likely not the only ones, nor possibly the best.
2. The fence of stereotypes, where one may make wide generalizations about one religion or the other.
3. The fence of prejudice, where an internal resentment of someone or something can flare out at someone else.[36]

Altemose goes on to say that these fences must be replaced with "bridges of acceptance, understanding, and tolerance . . . What another person considers sacred and holy demands respect simply because it is holy."[37]

As you discuss these issues, try not to prematurely judge each other or your beliefs. Listen to Paul's advice in 1 Corinthians 4:5: "[D]o not pronounce judgment before the time, before the Lord comes, who will

[35]Karl Keating, *Catholicism and Fundamentalism: The Attack on "Romanism" by "Bible Christians"* (San Francisco: Ignatius Press, 1988), 150.

[36]Altemose, *Why Do Catholics . . . ?*, 160.

[37]Ibid., 161.

bring to light the things now hidden in darkness and will disclose the purposes of the heart. Then each one will receive commendation from God."

In addition, as you work through this section, keep in mind that not all of your disagreements may be legitimate disagreements. "Misunderstandings, misrepresentations, and caricatures of one another . . . are not disagreements," say Colson and the other authors of "Evangelicals and Catholics Together."[38] You must strive to thoroughly understand the basis of each issue so you can work through any distortions and clearly identify with which points you agree or disagree based upon accurate information. Keep your lines of communication open so that you can talk about these sensitive issues without trampling the other person's religious beliefs. Remember that "a fool takes no pleasure in understanding, but only in expressing personal opinion" (Proverbs 18:2). By using tactfulness, sensitivity, and understanding in your discussions, you minimize the chances that harbored resentment will accumulate, which can weaken and perhaps even destroy your relationship.

The beliefs presented in this section of *United in Heart, Divided in Faith* are mostly Catholic beliefs and practices that are largely based on Catholic Church traditions, interpretations, or teachings because, although they are based in Scripture, no explicit guidelines for them appear in the Bible. The way Catholics incorporate these man-influenced or interpreted beliefs into their faith often causes difficulty for Protestants, whose belief system is *sola scriptura* or "based on the Bible alone."

I have strived to present balanced perspectives of each of the issues you will be discussing in this section. The goal is not to force either of you to accept any of these beliefs but to help you clearly understand the background of each of the beliefs. It is likely that, after finishing this section, you may agree to disagree regarding some or all of the beliefs presented. On the other hand, you may be surprised to find commonality within some of these differences, spiritually enriching your personal faith.

---

[37]Colson et al., "Evangelicals and Catholics Together."

DIFFERENCE 1

Catholic Use of Tradition in Conjunction with Scripture in Church Teachings

So then, brothers and sisters, stand firm and hold fast to the traditions that you were taught by us, either by word of mouth or by our letter (2 Thessalonians 2:15).

While both Catholics and Protestants believe in the infallibility of the Bible and the usefulness of the Bible "for teaching, for reproof, for correction, and for training in righteousness" (2 Timothy 3:16), Catholics believe that tradition is also an important way through which God teaches Christians. Because Protestants believe that all authority on God's teachings comes from and can be found within the Bible, they oppose this Catholic reliance on tradition. Consequently, the Catholic beliefs based upon traditions that fall outside the explicit contents of the Bible—beliefs that may have been inspired by the Holy Spirit but nonetheless involved some human interpretation—are those issues which normally cause conflicts between Catholics and Protestants and are likely the basis for many of the conflicts within your interfaith relationship.

Protestants may not know that the Catholic use of tradition in conjunction with Scripture doesn't oppose biblical teachings but is actually a biblical teaching itself, Catholics believe. In John 21:25, John says, "But there are also many other things that Jesus did; if every one of them were written down, I suppose that the world itself could not contain the books that would be written." How, then, are Christians supposed to learn what Jesus may have taught through his unrecorded actions if they haven't been written down? Through the inspiration of the Holy Spirit, Catholics respond. In Matthew 28:20, Jesus tells his disciples that his Spirit will remain with them even after he departs: " 'And remember, I am with you always, to the end of the age.' " And in John 14:26, Jesus explicitly describes to the apostles how God will send the Holy Spirit to continue to teach in his name: " 'But the Advocate, the Holy Spirit, whom the Father will send in my name, will teach you everything, and remind you of all that I have said to you.' " In this passage, Jesus seems to say that his Spirit will not only reinforce what he has already taught, as recorded in the Bible, but also teach "everything," implying that there are more truths than are contained in the Bible. Because the Catholic Church holds that the Catholic bishops are direct successors of the apostles (see page 155, "Sacrament of Holy Orders" in *Difference 7: Catholic Sacraments Described*), Catholics believe that the Catholic bishops can still receive the inspiration and guidance from the Holy Spirit that Jesus promised to the apostles. The *Catechism* elaborates:

> *"[Holy] Tradition transmits in its entirety the Word of God which has been entrusted to the apostles by Christ the Lord and the Holy Spirit. It transmits it to the successors of the apostles so that, enlightened by the Spirit of truth, they may faithfully preserve, expound, and spread it abroad by their preaching. . . .Both Scripture and Tradition must be accepted and honored with equal sentiments of devotion and reverence."* [39]

Catholics say that 2 Peter 1:20–21 also supports the role of tradition in Christian teaching: "[N]o prophesy of scripture is a matter of one's

---

[39] *CCC,* 81–82, quoting *Dei Verbum,* 9.

own interpretation, because no prophesy ever came by human will, but men and women moved by the Holy Spirit spoke from God." Catholics believe Peter is saying that in the same way that the Holy Spirit inspired the writing of Scripture, it must also inspire the interpretation of Scripture. These interpretations of Scripture, inspired by the Holy Spirit, have formed the basis for the traditions adhered to by the Catholic Church. Therefore, Catholics believe that all of their traditions are biblically grounded and based upon Spirit-inspired interpretations of Scripture.

In fact, Catholics note, the Christian church actually preceded the Bible, the Holy Spirit inspiring the writing of the Bible through the early church leaders, the apostles. But before the New Testament was even written, early Christians followed the oral teachings of the apostles: "They devoted themselves to the apostles' teaching and fellowship, to the breaking of bread and the prayers" (Acts 2:42). Right from the beginning of the church, Catholics believe, the "fullness of Christian teaching was found . . . in the Church as the living embodiment of Christ, not in a book."[40] Without oral tradition—an important component in Catholic traditional practices—the New Testament would never have been written.

Perhaps some of the Catholic-Protestant debates regarding the use of traditions are based on a misunderstanding of what Catholics mean as "tradition." By tradition, the Catholic Church is referring to "the body of unwritten knowledge given by Christ to the Apostles and handed down by them to their successors, the Church's bishops, who teach it to everybody else,"[41] truths that support the teaching of Christ. The kinds of traditions that are condemned in Scripture are human traditions, which oppose Christ's teaching or negate the Word of God. For example, in Colossians 2:8, Paul says, "See to it that no one takes you captive through philosophy and empty deceit, according to human tradition, according to the elemental spirits of the universe, and not according to Christ." And in Matthew 15:6–9, Jesus says, " 'So, for the sake of your

[40]Keating, *Catholicism and Fundamentalism,* 138.

[41]Kevin Orlin Johnson, *Expressions of the Catholic Faith* (New York: Ballantine Books, 1994), 3.

tradition, you make void the word of God. You hypocrites! Isaiah prophesied rightly about you when he said: " 'This people honors me with
their lips, but their hearts are far from me; in vain do they worship me,
teaching human precepts as doctrines.' " (Catholics are also often criticized for blindly participating in their traditions, most often the
sacraments, without faith, the type of practice condemned by Christ in
Matthew 15:6–9. Faith, however, is the crucial element in all of the
Catholic sacraments. See page 146, *Difference 7: Catholic Sacraments
Described.*)

Tradition comprises those beliefs that, though biblically based, are
not explicitly defined in Scripture, yet which, through the revelation of
the Holy Spirit, the Catholic Church believes are important in the lives
of Christians. No Catholic traditions will oppose God's commandments,
Christ's teachings, or biblical truths. All are intended to supplement the
truth and provide a richness to the glorification and worship of God and
his Son, Jesus Christ, through the inspiration of the Holy Spirit.

Catholics truly believe that Christ gave his Church authority to
receive and interpret inspirations from the Holy Spirit and to instruct its
members in these traditions inspired by the Spirit: " 'Whoever listens to
you listens to me, and whoever rejects you rejects me, and whoever
rejects me rejects the one who sent me' " (Luke 10:16). Not to follow
the Spirit-inspired traditions of the Church would be to reject Christ
himself, Catholics believe. In addition, following these traditions
adheres to biblical teachings such as 2 Thessalonians 3:6, which says to
"keep away from believers who are living in idleness and not according
to the tradition that they received from us." Catholics also believe that
through Isaiah 59:21, God promised the Church a living Spirit, who
inspires each tradition:

*And as for me, this is my covenant with them, says the Lord:
my spirit that is upon you, and my words that I have put in
your mouth, shall not depart out of your mouth, or out of the
mouths of your children, or out of the mouths of your
children's children, says the Lord, from now on and forever.*

Most Protestants oppose the Catholic use of tradition, believing in the authority of Scripture alone and being concerned about not knowing where to draw the line when accepting the authority of sources other than Scripture. When Paul referred to keeping the traditions that the apostles had taught, such as in 2 Thessalonians 3:6, Protestants assert that Paul was referring to things that had already been personally taught, not talking about traditions that might develop in the future. In their opposition of Catholic tradition, Protestants also cite biblical passages such as Deuteronomy 4:2 where Moses says, "You must neither add anything to what I command you nor take away anything from it, but keep the commandments of the Lord your God with which I am charging you." Protestants view Catholic traditions as adding to God's truth as contained in the Scripture. "By accepting Catholic Tradition as a means of divine revelation," say writers John Ankerberg and John Weldon, "even biblically correct teachings in the Church become hedged about with unbiblical trimmings, which in turn tend to either revise, neutralize, or nullify these truths."[42]

A way to evaluate Catholic traditions as you discuss them within your interfaith relationship is to use the same guidelines that John gave us for testing spirits: "By this you know the Spirit of God: every spirit that confesses that Jesus Christ has come in the flesh is from God, and every spirit that does not confess Jesus is not from God" (1 John 4:2–3). Use this biblical truth as the means against which to evaluate each Catholic traditional teaching. Because Jesus only wants us to follow those traditions that don't oppose his teachings or God's commandments, if a particular tradition can give glory to Jesus Christ, then by biblical standards, it isn't opposing God and can therefore be followed. This evaluation measure may be helpful in bringing each tradition into a biblical context with which you are both comfortable and familiar, making it easier for you to discuss the tradition. As you work through the chapters in the rest of this section, keep in mind that each tradition must be able to glorify Jesus as Lord in order to be valid.

---

[42]John Ankerberg and John Weldon, *The Facts on Roman Catholicism* (Eugene, Ore.: Harvest House Publishers, 1993), 5.

In your discussions, also remember this very important point: In order to be saved, traditions are not needed. All that is needed is a personal commitment to Jesus Christ as your Lord and Savior and the desire to do his will in your lives: " 'Everyone who calls on the name of the Lord shall be saved' " (Romans 10:13).

Relationship Builders

• Catholics believe that both Scripture and tradition are sources of truth in the life of a Christian.
How do we each feel about the Catholic Church's teachings based largely on tradition?
Does a particular belief or practice have to be explicitly defined in Scripture for either of us to accept it? Why or why not?

• The Bible talks about good tradition that glorifies God and bad tradition that doesn't involve, or opposes, God.
In what category would each of us place Catholic Church traditions?
How have our education and experience impacted how we approach the use or nonuse of tradition in religious teachings?

• Most Protestants believe that the Catholic use of tradition adds to Scripture, a practice forbidden in the Bible.
Why might Protestants be concerned about the possibility of the Catholic Church adding to biblical truth through its traditions?
Does either of us feel that the Catholic Church is misleading its members by teachings beliefs that, though grounded in Scripture, are still largely based in tradition?

• Evaluating traditions using John's measures for evaluating spirits may make discussing traditions easier.
Do we agree that a traditional teaching that glorifies God may be valid?
Would it work for us to use John's guidelines in evaluating Catholic beliefs based in tradition as well as in Scripture?

DIFFERENCE 2

Catholic Devotion to Mary

*And [Gabriel] came to her and said, "Greetings, favored one!
The Lord is with you"* (Luke 1:28).

*And Elizabeth was filled with the Holy Spirit and exclaimed
with a loud cry, "Blessed are you among women, and blessed
is the fruit of your womb"* (Luke 1:41–42).

These passages from Scripture are the basis for the popular Catholic prayer, the "Hail Mary." Many Protestants may know of this prayer, yet may not realize that its words are rooted in Scripture. And this is only one of many misunderstandings on the parts of both Protestants and Catholics concerning Mary, the mother of Jesus. In my personal experience as a Catholic, I have heard more arguments from Protestants relating to Marian issues than any other difference between Catholics and Protestants. Likely, these issues are causing some tension in your interfaith relationship as well.

In his introduction to a chapter about Mary in *Catholic and Christian*, Schreck summarizes the problems concerning the attention Catholics give to Mary, some of which you may recognize as being points of conflict in your own relationship:

> *It is a tragic fact that beliefs about Mary, the mother of Jesus,
> have become a source of division among Christians. Many
> Christians honestly do not understand what Catholics believe*

about Mary and why. Sometimes Catholics have been accused of worshipping Mary. For their part, many Catholics do not understand why other Christians are sensitive to the attention given to Mary by Catholics. Indeed, many Catholics do not understand what their own church teaches about Mary and are thus ill-equipped to explain these beliefs to others.[43]

"As a Protestant growing up, I was taught by some that Catholics worship Mary as a sort of demigod," says Brian. "My perception was reinforced by popular media in which Catholics were seen elevating statues of Mary while chanting and praying to Mary. I was also taught that the early Catholic Church under Constantine wanted to make Christianity more appealing for pagans, so it deliberately incorporated the worship of Mary into its doctrine, reflecting that day's pagan worship of the goddesses Venus [Aphrodite] and Diana [Artemis]."

This chapter will present why Catholics have what they refer to as a "devotion" to Mary, an honor recognizing Mary's acceptance and fulfillment of the role of the mother of Jesus through which she put God's will ahead of any personal reservations. This devotion is not the same as the "worship" or "adoration" offered to God.

As a basis for discussing these Marian issues, it may be helpful to establish what common beliefs Catholics and Protestants hold when it comes to Mary. Both Catholics and Protestants believe that Mary fulfilled an extremely important role when she, as a virgin, willingly told the archangel Gabriel that she would bear God's son, fulfilling Isaiah's prophesy that " the young woman is with child and shall bear a son, and shall name him Immanuel" (Isaiah 7:14). In the "Roman Catholicism" chapter of *Fast Facts on False Teachings*, authors Ron Carlson and Ed Decker elaborate on the Protestant perspective of Mary:

As Protestants we do recognize Mary in a very special way. We honor Mary as the mother of our Lord, Jesus Christ. As Christians we believe what the Bible says: that Mary was blessed to bear Jesus. She was a humble maidservant, a

---

[43]Schreck, *Catholic and Christian,* 163.

---

servant of God who submitted herself to God and gave birth to the Savior. We honor her for this.[44]

Protestants and Catholics alike, therefore, respect Mary for her willingness to carry out God's will in her own life. Catholics, however, carry this respect into devotion because Mary's perfect response to God has made her a model for the Catholic Church, an example of how all Christians should respond to God.

In addition to her being the model for the Church, the Catholic Church feels special devotion should be given to Mary because of her role in man's salvation. In his letter to the Galatians, Paul refers to Mary's role in the birth of Jesus: "But when the fullness of time had come, God sent his Son, born of a woman, born under the law, in order to redeem those who were under the law, so that we might receive adoption as children" (Galatians 4:4–5). Through her acceptance of the role of Jesus' mother, even as an unmarried woman, Mary enabled God's son to be born and ultimately to die for the salvation of all. The Catholic Church does acknowledge, however, that Mary's role in man's salvation was only as intermediary, essentially the means through which the Savior was sent to mankind. Her role—though small—was vital, and one for which the Catholic Church believes she should be honored.

The Catholic Church points out that the devotion offered to Mary differs essentially from the worship offered to God, supporting and uplifting this worship. To explain this distinction, the Catholic Church turns to Latin, where the worship offered only to God is called *latria* and is distinctly different from *hyperdulia,* the reverence or respect that is given to Mary. (*Dulia,* respect given to other Catholic saints, will be discussed in *Difference 4: Praying for the Help of Mary and Other Saints* on page 128.)

Most Protestants aren't satisfied with these Latin explanations. In *Roman Catholics and Evangelicals: Agreements and Differences,* authors Norman L. Geisler and Ralph E. MacKenzie say that "despite theological distinctions to the contrary, in practice there is often no real

---

[44]Ron Carlson and Ed Decker, *Fast Facts on False Teachings* (Eugene, Oreg.: Harvest House Publishers, 1994), 221.

difference between the veneration given to Mary and that given to Christ."[45] In spite of Catholic Church teachings to the contrary, Protestants believe that most Catholics pray to Mary as they would to God, thinking that they are doing what the Catholic Church requires.

And Protestants may have a point. Even though "worshipping" Mary is against the official teachings of the Catholic Church, some Catholics likely are zealous in their devotion to Mary. However, Protestants may see this characteristic displayed in some people—and even through the media, as my husband did—and then incorrectly assume that each Catholic responds to Mary in this way. Therefore, it is the active responsibility of the Catholic to knowingly differentiate his or her devotion to Mary from his or her worship of God. And it is the responsibility of the Protestant to understand the official Catholic position concerning devotion to Mary and to recognize deviations from this devotion for what they are—deviations.

In approaching your perspective of Mary, it may be helpful to keep in mind what I once heard a priest say. He reminded us that Mary was Jesus' mother, where Jesus had similar feelings for her and love for her as we have for our own mothers. And like we want others to treat our mothers with love and respect, Jesus wants us to treat his mother with love and respect, adhering to the commandment to "Honor . . . your mother, as the Lord your God commanded you" (Deut. 5:16). While some Catholics may be guilty of giving too much attention to Mary, some Protestants often seem to err in the other direction, denouncing Mary to avoid committing what they perceive to be the sin of idolatry. We need to remember that just as Christians are brothers and sisters of Christ, Mary, as Jesus' mother, is also our spiritual mother.

Jesus confirmed the mother-child relationship he desires for his mother and all Christians, Catholics believe, when he was hanging on the cross and he said to his mother, " 'Woman, here is your son,' " and to the apostle John, " 'Here is your mother,' " (John 19:26). You need to remember to honor Mary because God has honored her by choosing her to be the mother of Jesus." Whether you decide to translate this honor

---

[45]Norman L. Geisler and Ralph E. MacKenzie, *Roman Catholics and Evangelicals, Agreements and Differences* (Grand Rapids, Mich.: Baker Books, 1995), 322.

into a passive respect or an active, devotional respect, however, is a personal decision that you will each have to make.

Relationship Builders

• Catholics and Protestants both respect Mary for submitting herself to God and agreeing to be the mother of Jesus.
   In our religious upbringing, what was each of us taught about Mary?
   Do we still hold the same beliefs that we were taught?

• The Catholic Church believes devotion should be given to Mary because of her perfect response to God, and also because of her role in man's salvation.
   Do we agree that Mary is a good model for a Christian?
   Do we believe that she had an active role in man's salvation? Why or why not?
   Are these attributes and actions for which honor or devotion should be given to her?

• Using Latin terms, the Catholic Church very specifically differentiates between reverence given to Mary *(hyperdulia)* and worship given to God *(latria)*.
   Do we both believe these distinctions are actually adhered to by Catholics? Or does either of us feel that the distinction between the two is too ambiguous, resulting in Catholics truly "worshipping" Mary?

DIFFERENCE 3

Other Marian Issues

And Mary said, "My soul magnifies the Lord, and my spirit rejoices in God my Savior, for he has looked with favor on the lowliness of his servant. Surely, from now on all generations will call me blessed; for the Mighty One has done great things for me, and holy is his name" (Luke 1:46–49).

The Catholic devotion to Mary discussed in the previous chapter is only one of the Marian beliefs that differ between Catholics and Protestants. Although based in Scripture, most of these beliefs aren't explicitly defined in Scripture and are instead based on tradition, pope decrees, or other circumstances in which men other than the apostles have had an influence, causing difficulties for many Protestants. Other differences in beliefs arise out of various interpretations of Scripture between Catholics and Protestants. Although these beliefs about Mary are important, they shouldn't be a source of division in your relationship. Nonetheless, you still need to have a clear understanding of these beliefs, so here are both the Catholic and Protestant views of:

- Mary as the Immaculate Conception
- Mary's Sinlessness
- Mary's Bodily Assumption Into Heaven
- Mary's Title of Mother of God

- Mary's Perpetual Virginity
- Mary's Apparitions and Appearances

Mary as the Immaculate Conception

The "Immaculate Conception" is the Catholic belief that Mary was preserved from original sin from the moment of her conception. It is not, as some think, a description of the way in which Jesus was conceived by the Holy Spirit in Mary's womb.

Catholic view: This Catholic belief is rooted in Scripture, including Gabriel's greeting of Mary as "favored one" (Luke 1:28)—or "full of grace" in other translations—this perfect greeting only being perfect, as Catholic scholar Ludwig Ott says, "if it extends over her whole life, beginning with her entry into the world."[46] In defense of this belief, Catholics also cite Luke 1:42 where Elizabeth says, " 'Blessed are you among women, and blessed is the fruit of your womb,' " drawing what Catholics say is a parallel between the sinlessness of Christ and the sinlessness of his mother.

Also supporting the Catholic belief in the Immaculate Conception is the human rationalization among early Christians that "it would have been impossible for Mary to respond as she did, and for God to dwell within her, unless God had given her a remarkable, special grace."[47] Catholics also acknowledge, however, that as a human, Mary too needed Christ as her Savior. She was simply the first whom he saved, being saved before her conception.

A belief in Mary as the Immaculate Conception was defined as an official teaching of the Catholic Church by Pope Pius IX in 1854 and is celebrated in the Catholic Church on December 8.

Protestant view: Protestants reject the belief in Mary's Immaculate Conception, primarily because they believe that Scripture does not support the belief and feel that it is based primarily on Catholic Church

---

[46]Ludwig Ott, *Fundamentals of Catholic Dogma,* ed. James Canon Bastible, trans. Patrick Lynch (Rockford, Ill.: Tan Books and Publishers, 1960), 200, quoted in Geisler and MacKenzie, *Roman Catholics and Evangelicals,* 305.

[47]Schreck, *Catholic and Christian,* 177.

tradition. In referring to the argument that Mary was the first to be saved, albeit before her conception, Protestants hold that there is no biblical evidence for it. In addition, they say that it is unbiblical to teach that a person could be saved before conception, before placing faith in Christ. Furthermore, Protestants claim that this teaching is contrary to Mary's own confession that God was her Savior (Luke 1:47) after her conception.

Mary's Sinlessness

Catholics believe that Mary was not only sinless at her conception but also remained sinless for the rest of her life.

Catholic view: Theologians in the early church began raising the possibility that Mary was sinless. Saint Augustine for one questioned, "How do we know what abundance of grace for the total overcoming of sin was conferred upon her, who merited to conceive and bear him in whom there was no sin?"[48] In support of this belief, Catholics again cite Gabriel's calling Mary "full of grace," where, Catholics say, he was referring to her sinless state. In addition, Christians know how much God hates sin. If God abhors sin, Catholics would argue, how could he be conceived within the womb of a woman bearing sin? The only conclusion for Catholics, then, is that Mary was sinless all her life.

Protestant view: Protestants say that the Bible does not support Mary's sinlessness, citing again Luke 1:47 where Mary calls God her Savior. Referring to Gabriel's greeting of Mary, Protestants say that Gabriel was referring to her present state of blessedness, not to her whole life as being sinless and that the grace God gave her was for becoming Jesus' mother, not to keep her from sinning. Further, Ott acknowledges that many "Greek Fathers (Origen, Saint Basil, Saint John Chrysostom, Saint Cyril of Alexander) taught that Mary suffered from venial personal faults, such as ambition and vanity, doubt about the message of the Angel, and lack of faith under the Cross,"[49] which would mean that she wasn't entirely sinless.

---

[48] Augustine of Hippo, "Nature and Grace," 36, 42, in *The Faith of the Early Fathers,* vol. 3, 111, quoted in Schreck, *Catholic and Christian,* 177.

[49] Ott, *Fundamentals of Catholic Dogma,* 203, quoted in Geisler and MacKenzie, *Roman Catholics and Evangelicals,* 310.

Mary's Bodily Assumption into Heaven

This Catholic belief, which emerged among early Christians, says that when Mary reached the end of her earthly life, she was assumed both body and soul into heaven. This differs from Christ's ascension into heaven under his own power; Mary was assumed into heaven through the power of God.

Catholic view: Like the Immaculate Conception, Catholics say, Mary's bodily assumption is an example of how Mary received in advance the assumption of the body that will happen to all believers at the final judgment. The basis for this belief is mainly early church teachings that God would not want the body that held his son to undergo decay and, because of her sinless state, Mary's body would be excluded from the decay of the body that results from sin. Tradition also holds that, right before her death, the apostles gathered around Mary and prayed that God would take her both body and soul into heaven, and God answered their prayer. The belief in Mary's assumption was declared by Pope Pius XII in 1950 and is celebrated by the Catholic Church on August 15.

Protestant view: Because Protestants don't normally believe in Mary's Immaculate Conception or her sinlessness, the Catholic arguments based on these beliefs don't convince them that Mary was assumed into heaven. And nowhere in the Bible is an account given of Mary's assumption into heaven, an event that would have been a miracle and, therefore, should have been recorded by at least the disciple John, who outlived all of the other disciples. Because support for Mary's assumption doesn't explicitly appear in Scripture, Protestants regard this teaching as unverifiable and therefore don't typically accept this doctrine.

Mary's Title of "Mother of God"

The early church first gave Mary the titles of *Christotokos*, meaning "Mother of Christ" and *Theotokos*, meaning "God-bearer" or "Mother of God," acknowledging that Mary was the mother of him who was both wholly man and wholly God. Some Protestants object to calling Mary the Mother of God, feeling that it could incorrectly attribute Jesus' divinity to Mary.

Catholic view: Because Jesus was both man and God, Catholics say that it is appropriate to refer to his mother, Mary, as both the Mother of Christ and the Mother of God. Elizabeth even used this title when greeting Mary: " 'And why has this happened to me, that the mother of my Lord comes to me?' " (Luke 1:43). The Catholic Church points out that the title "Mother of God" recognizes Mary as the one from whom the incarnate God took his human flesh and should not imply that Mary was the source of Christ's divinity.

Protestant view: Many Protestants hesitate to refer to Mary as the Mother of God because they don't want to attribute Jesus' human and divine natures to Mary, nor do they want to elevate Mary to a level tantamount to and parallel to God. It is interesting to note, however, that both Luther and John Calvin used this title in referring to Mary.[50]

Mary's Perpetual Virginity

Although Catholics and Protestants agree that Mary was a virgin when she conceived and gave birth to Jesus, Catholics believe that Mary remained a virgin her entire life while most Protestants say she went on to have four sons and a few daughters, half-brothers and half-sisters of Jesus.

Catholic view: The Catholic Church says that Mary freely chose to retain her virginity throughout her entire life to honor God. This belief was taught by church leaders of the fourth century and earlier. And early Protestant reformers, including Luther and Calvin, believed Mary's virginity continued after the birth of Christ, citing in part Ezekiel 44:2, which could refer to Mary's womb being "closed" after Christ's birth: "The Lord said to me: This gate shall remain shut; it shall not be opened, and no one shall enter by it; for the Lord, the God of Israel, has entered by it; therefore it shall remain shut."[51]

---

[50]Geisler and MacKenzie, Roman Catholics and Evangelicals, 299.

[51]Chris Tesch, "The Perpetual Virginity of Mary," www.catholic-defense.com/mary.htm, 2002. Accessed 15 Sept. 2002.

Regarding the biblical references to Jesus' brothers and sisters, such as Matthew 13:55–56, Catholics say that in the Bible, the Greek words for "brothers" and "sisters" were also used to refer to other close relatives such as cousins, therefore not proving that these were Mary's children. For example, in the Septuagint (the Greek translation of the Hebrew Old Testament), Lot is referred to as the brother of Abraham using the Greek word for brother, *adelphos,* when Lot was really Abraham's nephew, as indicated in Genesis 11:27. Others say that Jesus' brothers and sisters could have been Joseph's children from a previous marriage, maintaining Mary's virginity.

Protestant view: Even though Luther believed that Mary remained a virgin after the birth of Christ,[52] Protestants argue that there are numerous clear references to Jesus' brothers and sisters in the Bible, proving that Mary and Joseph had other children after Jesus. Protestants also cite Matthew 1:25 as evidence that Mary and Joseph had normal married sexual relations after the birth of Jesus: "But [Joseph] had no marital relations with her until she had borne a son; and he named him Jesus." And various biblical passages attest that sex is an essential part of marriage, including Genesis 1:28, where God told Adam and Eve to " 'be fruitful and multiply.' " Joseph and Mary's marriage is no exception, Protestants argue.

Even though Catholics and Protestants may debate over the perpetual virginity of Mary, both Catholic and Protestant scholars say that the Bible doesn't provide enough evidence to support or deny Mary's perpetual virginity. Furthermore, Luther said this belief "neither adds nor detracts from faith. It is immaterial whether these men were Christ's cousins or his [half-] brothers begotten by Joseph"[53] You too should be careful not to let this or other Marian beliefs cause discord within your interfaith relationship.

---

[52]Ibid., 301.

[53]Eric W. Gritsch, "The Views of Luther and Lutheranism on the Veneration of Mary," in *The One Mediator, The Saints, and Mary—Lutherans and Catholics in Dialogue VIII,* ed. H. George Anderson (Minneapolis: Augsburg, 1992), 239, quoted in Geisler and MacKenzie, *Roman Catholics and Evangelicals,* 301–302.

Mary's Apparitions and Appearances

This chapter on Marian beliefs would not be complete without at least mentioning Mary's alleged appearances throughout the years. Although most of these appearances are dismissed by the Catholic Church as hoaxes, certain appearances have been established as genuine, including her appearances at Guadalupe, Mexico, in 1531; Lourdes, France, in 1858; and Fatima, Portugal, in 1981.

Catholic view: Of perhaps all of the Marian appearances, Mary's 1858 appearance to Saint Bernadette near Lourdes, France, is probably the most famous and compelling for Catholics. Through eighteen visits with fourteen-year-old Bernadette Soubirous, Mary referred to herself as the Immaculate Conception and revealed a spring, which many attest has supernatural healing powers. The majority of Catholics respect the Catholic Church's authority in evaluating which appearances of Mary are genuine and listen to the messages which she delivers through these appearances, often urging people to pray, turn away from sin, and convert their lives to God.

Protestant view: Protestants typically dismiss these alleged appearances of Mary as false. Protestants also claim that the messages delivered by these apparitions fail to exalt Jesus, which is why they are also dismissed. Some even believe that these apparitions are actually manifestations of Satan and his demons, knowing that "even Satan disguises himself as an angel of light" (2 Corinthians 11:14).

Relationship Builders

* Most Catholic beliefs about Mary are primarily based on tradition and other interpretations of man.
  What are our perspectives of these Marian beliefs since they aren't explicitly defined in Scripture?
  Does their lack of undeniable biblical basis cause either of us to completely disregard them as false?

- The Marian beliefs explained in this chapter are:

  Mary as the Immaculate Conception—Mary was conceived without sin.

  Mary's Sinlessness—Mary did not sin throughout her entire life.

  Mary's Bodily Assumption into Heaven—At her death, Mary was taken into heaven body and soul.

  Mary's Title "Mother of God"—Mary is recognized as the mother of her Son Jesus, who is wholly man and wholly God.

  Mary's Perpetual Virginity—Mary remained a virgin throughout her life.

  Mary's Apparitions and Appearances—Mary has appeared to select individuals to deliver specific messages.

  What opinions do we have regarding each of these Marian beliefs?

- Some Marian beliefs are core Christian beliefs. But while Catholics and Protestants believe differently about Mary, a couple shouldn't let these beliefs cause conflicts and damage within their interfaith relationship.

  Have any of our relationship conflicts centered on our differences regarding beliefs in Mary?

  What attitude does each of us hold toward Mary? Have these attitudes caused conflicts in our relationship?

  What steps could we take to resolve these conflicts?

DIFFERENCE 4

Praying for the Help of Mary and Other Saints

Likewise the Spirit helps us in our weakness; for we do not know how to pray as we ought, but that very Spirit intercedes with sighs too deep for words. And God, who searches the heart, knows what is the mind of the Spirit, because the Spirit intercedes for the saints according to the will of God (Romans 8:26–27).

From the time he was a little boy, my husband has loved airplanes, so a career in aviation was a natural choice for him. Early in his career, he had received a job offer to be a flight instructor at a small, local airport. A few days after he had started this job, however, he was offered a managerial position at another airport. After much thought, he decided to accept the second offer and called his first boss to explain the situation. This man had a few choice words for Brian and, suffice it to say, would not be a good future reference for him! So after business hours one evening, Brian and I went to the airport to retrieve the few personal items he had left in his desk. But one thing was missing: his flight logbook.

For those of you not familiar with aviation, a pilot's flight logbook is the indispensable record of each and every hour that the pilot has flown. Without it, a pilot cannot get hired. And now Brian's logbook was missing.

Not knowing what to do, I remembered advice my great-grand-mother had given me when I was young: When something is lost, ask Saint Anthony, who assists in finding lost things, to help you. So that's what I did. I asked Saint Anthony to lead me to wherever the logbook was. I stumbled across the small office, climbed on top of a chair, and began thumbing through books on a high bookshelf. I pulled out a thin, black book—the logbook! What happened, we think, is that after getting Brian's resignation call, his angered boss had gone into Brian's desk, taken his logbook, and hidden it for spite. Needless to say, Brian was quite surprised that I had found it, albeit skeptical of my method.

"While I don't think that Saint Anthony or his fellow saints had anything to do with finding the logbook," says Brian, "I'll admit that her search was unorthodox but still successful."

I believe that the Holy Spirit interceded on my behalf, delivering to God my prayers joined with those of Saint Anthony. God then answered our prayers by revealing the location of the logbook to me.

The Protestant readers will probably react to this story with the same skepticism that Brian did because Protestants typically don't believe in asking dead saints for help for a variety of reasons. But what may surprise both Protestants and Catholics is that this belief is rooted in a practice that is advocated by both denominations: intercessory prayer.

Catholics and Protestants both believe that the Holy Spirit is the one intercessor for us in our prayers. Catholics and Protestants also acknowledge that "there is also one mediator between God and humankind, Christ Jesus" (1 Timothy 2:5). Catholics and Protestants acknowledge that no person, living or dead, can ever fill these roles of God the Son and God the Holy Spirit. That being said, Catholics and Protestants both believe in the power of intercessory prayer: asking friends, family, and sometimes even strangers to pray to God for special intentions, healing, guidance, or a myriad other requests. Many Christians participate in "prayer chains," networks of people who let one another know special intentions about which to pray. Samuel even views intercessory prayer as an obligation, saying, " '[A]s for me, far be it from me that I should sin against the Lord by ceasing to pray for you'" (1 Samuel 12:23). In asking saints for prayers, Catholics are taking their requests for intercessory prayer to those who are already in heaven. Catholics believe that the saints in heaven are as much part of the body of Christ as any living Christian and can therefore pray for us just as anyone on earth can.

From the Catholic perspective, in no way are requests for prayers from saints intended to detract from the worship owed to only God alone. On the contrary, these prayers are intended to bring one closer to God. In Hebrews 12:1, the author says that "we are surrounded by so great a cloud of witnesses," which the Catholic Church believes refers in part to the deceased saints. The Catholic Church also encourages its members to model their lives after those of the saints, much as Paul says to do in 1 Corinthians 11:1: "Be imitators of me, as I am of Christ." Catholics believe they can do this through devotion to saints, which is getting to know the saints through prayer and imitating the virtues of those who are already with God. All prayers directed toward Mary or any other saint are intended to bring a person in closer connection with Almighty God.

What may be confusing is that Catholics often use the phrase "pray to" when they are referring to asking saints for prayers. This phrase is used because the way in which a person communicates with a saint (silent or spoken words) is similar to the way in which one prays to God. The *form* of communicating is the only similarity, however. Catholics do not pray to Mary and the other saints as they pray to God. In explaining this distinction, the Catholic Church turns to Latin terms, which were mentioned in *Difference 2: Catholic Devotion to Mary* on page 115. Worship of God is called *latria*, while respect of the saints is called *dulia,* and the reverence offered to Mary, who holds a special place among the saints, is called *hyperdulia.*

In spite of these official distinctions, many Protestants still view the practice of "praying to" saints as being blasphemous and idolatrous. Because prayer is an act of religious devotion and a type of worship, any form of prayer offered to anyone or anything other than God violates this commandment: "[Y]ou shall have no other gods before me" (Exodus 20:3). Furthermore, as was also stated in the previous chapter on pages 117–118, most Protestants believe that Catholics make no distinction in their personal worship of God and devotion to the saints, regardless of official distinctions taught by the Catholic Church.

Even though Protestants believe in intercessory prayer offered by living people on earth, they generally don't believe in asking dead saints for prayers. Protestants point out that God is the only one who can be omnipresent and omniscient. It wouldn't be possible, then, for a particular saint to receive prayer requests from all over the world at the same time. In addition, some Protestants believe that going to a saint with a request questions the effectiveness of Christ's role as mediator. And in Romans 8:26, Paul tells us that the Spirit intercedes for us. If we have God as our intercessor, why would we need other spiritual intercessors, such as the saints, Protestants ask.

Another reason some Protestants object to the Catholic practice of speaking to saints is that, through this practice, Catholics are essentially communicating with the dead, and communication with the dead—such as through a medium—is a form of occultism that is forbidden by the Bible. For example, in Deuteronomy 18:10–11, Moses says, "No one shall be found among you who . . . consults ghosts or spirits, or who seeks oracles from the dead." And Isaiah warns, "Now if people say to you, 'Consult the ghosts and the familiar spirits that chirp and mutter; should not a people consult their gods, the dead on behalf of the living, for teaching and for instruction?' Surely, those who speak like this will have no dawn!" (Isaiah 8:19–20). However, Catholics too reject all types of divination, fortune-telling, and other practices related to the occult. Catholics say that their prayers to saints are different from the biblically denounced type of communication with the dead that a medium would invoke, but Protestants generally have trouble seeing that distinction.

As you can see from this discussion, the debate over praying to Mary and the other saints is much like a tennis match, where each side has what they believe to be a compelling reason for accepting or rejecting each facet of this practice. Again, you may not be able to agree regarding your stance on this issue, but at least make the effort to understand the issue from each other's perspective.

Relationship Builders

- Catholics and Protestant both believe in the sufficiency of Jesus as the one mediator between God and men and in the Holy Spirit as the one intercessor.

  Can we see how the Catholic belief in asking saints for prayers supports the biblical truths of Jesus as the one mediator and the Holy Spirit as the one intercessor, or does this practice seem to contradict the Bible?

- Catholics and Protestants both believe in the power of intercessory prayer.

  Do we pray for others and, in turn, ask others to pray for us or our loved ones?

  Have we experienced any miracles in our lives that we can attribute to intercessory prayer?

  Is any aspect of our interfaith relationship related to intercessory prayer?

- Catholics believe that their devotions to the saints are another form of intercessory prayer and do not conflict with their worship of God.

  Can we appreciate the Catholic perspective that asking saints in heaven for prayers is like asking those living on earth to pray for us?

  Or does either of us feel that speaking with saints is a type of occultism forbidden by the Bible?

- Protestants typically oppose the practice of "praying to" saints because they view it as blasphemous, idolatrous, related to the occult, and offensive to both Jesus' role as mediator and the intercession of the Holy Spirit.

What perspective have we each had regarding the Catholic devotion to saints?

Has our perspective changed at all after working through this chapter?

If our perspectives are different, how has that difference impacted our interfaith relationship?

DIFFERENCE 5

Justification

But now, apart from law, the righteousness of God has been disclosed, and is attested by the law and the prophets, the righteousness of God through faith in Jesus Christ for all who believe. For there is no distinction, since all have sinned and fall short of the glory of God; they are now justified by his grace as a gift, through the redemption that is in Christ Jesus, whom God put forward as a sacrifice of atonement by his blood, effective through faith (Romans 3:21–25).

S aint Paul states in his letter to the Romans that God's righteousness, or justice, which was revealed in the law, is now revealed to everyone who believes in Jesus Christ. We are redeemed by Jesus and are justified through the free gift of his grace. Catholics and Protestants do hold many of the same beliefs regarding justification, but the differences are what have sparked many Catholic-Protestant debates. Some of the disagreements are due to genuine theological belief differences, but some may also be due to the use of different words and phrases and other misunderstandings, which will be presented in this chapter.

Like many of the disagreements between Catholics and Protestants, the conflict concerning justification has its roots in the Protestant Reformation which began in the sixteenth century. Protestants were united by the common belief of "justification by faith alone" (*sola fide*), which they believed wasn't supported by the Catholic Church with its emphasis on faith combined with works leading to justification and salvation. If you have found seeds of this issue creating disagreements within your interfaith relationship, your best approach is to correctly understand both the Catholic and Protestant viewpoints so that, as with other issues, you can find your commonalties and understand your differences.

Let's start by laying on the table those beliefs that Catholics and Protestants hold in common regarding justification. Both believe that justification is a free gift from God, out of his grace, attainable through faith alone. Both believe that through the gift of justification we are liberated from the dominating power of sin and accepted into communion with God, already now, but then fully in God's coming kingdom. (Romans 5:1ff). Catholics and Protestants see justification as a condition that leads us to salvation, that it occurs in the reception of the Holy Spirit in Baptism and that it comes from God alone through faith in the gospel of God's Son. Both believe that justification is conversion, turning toward God and away from sin.

Now the differences.

Some Protestants believe that justification is only necessary once in a lifetime and, along with salvation, cannot be lost, despite any sins a person may commit. This doctrine is based on passages such as Isaiah 43:25, which says, "I am He who blots out your transgressions for my own sake, and I will not remember your sins," and Psalm 32:1–2, "Happy are those whose transgression is forgiven, whose sin is covered. Happy are those to whom the Lord imputes no iniquity, and in whose spirit there is no deceit." Other Protestants believe that justification and salvation can be lost due to sin but can be regained through confession of sins and contrition for sins through the grace of God.

Most Protestants also believe that if they have been justified, then they are assured of their salvation. If one has received Christ, he or she, without a doubt, will live with God forever in glory, a belief based on passages such as John 3:36, "Whoever believes in the Son has eternal life," and John 5:24, " 'Very truly, I tell you, anyone who hears my word and believes him who sent me has eternal life, and does not come under judgment, but has passed from death to life.' "

Catholics too believe that faith alone is the root of justification. Catholics believe they are initially justified as infants during the sacrament of Baptism through the faith of their parents (or, in the case of adult baptism, through personal faith), but this justification—and salvation—can be lost due to mortal sin. As adults, Catholics can regain justification that has been lost through repentance and sorrow expressed while receiving God's grace through the sacrament of Reconciliation.

Even after they are justified, Catholics are hopeful that they will live eternally with God but don't know for sure until death and judgment because the person's eternal destiny depends on the person's state of sin, or state of grace, at death. If a person dies in a state of "mortal" sin, the sin would have caused the person to lose justification and salvation, and that person would be condemned to hell. If a person dies in a state of "venial" sin, the person may enter purgatory for purification before entering heaven. (See page 151, "Sacrament of Reconciliation" in *Difference 7: Catholic Sacraments Described* for more about mortal and venial sins.) In support of this belief, Catholics cite Paul's uncertainty of his salvation in spite of his belief in Christ: "I am not aware of anything against myself, but I am not thereby acquitted. It is the Lord who judges me" (1 Corinthians 4:4).

Some of the disagreements between Protestants and Catholics regarding justification come from the different ways in which each uses the word "justification." For example, the Catholic belief that justification can be lost and regained has been referred to as receiving a "second justification" or "progressive justification," incorrectly implying for some that justification is something that can increase or decrease based on a person's actions, which is unbiblical. The misperception here is that what some refer to as a Catholic belief in second or progressive justification is actually the Catholic belief in sanctification and growth in righteousness, which is also a belief that Protestants hold. *The Catholic Encyclopedia* explains how "justification" is sometimes used to describe the sanctification process: "The increase of grace is by theologians justly called a second justification . . . , as distinct from the first justification . . . which is coupled with a remission of sin; for, though there be in the second justification no transit from sin to grace, there is an advance from grace to more perfect sharing therein."[54]

Sanctification, the process of growing in righteousness, begins when a person is justified, being regenerated, or born again, and receiving the "righteousness from God based on faith" (Philippians 3:9). Because Christ's sacrifice fulfilled God's law, making man right with God, this righteousness of Christ replaces our sinful nature through justification. A justified person is now the "temple of the Holy Spirit" (1 Corinthians 6:19) and is being "renewed in knowledge according to the image of its creator" (Colossians 3:10). Graham elaborates, "When we accept Jesus Christ as our Savior, He comes into our hearts and lives, cleanses us from sin, and makes a home in us. At that moment we begin to grow into the likeness of Christ, . . . and we continue to grow until that moment when we go to be with Christ and receive our glorified bodies."[55] Catholics believe that sanctification occurs by means of "sanctifying grace," a gift that perfects the soul and prepares it to live with God, and see the Catholic sacraments as having a role in sanctification. Sanctification, not justification, can increase or decrease.

An understanding of the similar Catholic-Protestant belief in sanctification may help to clarify the debate regarding the role of works in justification and salvation. Because Protestants believe in justification and salvation solely by faith, they feel that Catholics have made a serious theological error when they stress the importance of works for one's justification and salvation. Catholics respond by citing passages such as James 2:17: "So faith by itself, if it has no works, is dead." Both Catholics and Protestants believe that a genuine faith in Christ is what justifies. Catholics further describe the kind of genuine faith that can justify as being the type of faith that is active in charity and good works. By associating faith with works for justification and salvation, Catholics are saying that only through genuine faith can we be justified and saved, and if indeed this faith is genuine, it will unequivocally result in good works. And as was presented on page 53 in *Belief 7: We Believe*

[54]"Sanctifying Grace" in *The Catholic Encyclopedia,* vol. VI, trans. Scott Anthony Hibbs and Wendy Lorraine Hoffman, 1999, www.newadvent.org/cathen/06701a.htm. Accessed 20 Sept. 2002.

[55]Graham, *Unto the Hills,* 102.

in Performing Good Works to Outwardly Reflect Our Inner Faith, Protestants believe works of charity will flow from this type of genuine faith as well. Catholics, like Protestants, don't believe that one can perform works to earn justification or salvation. But through genuine faith, we are justified and saved. And the consequence, or outpouring, of this genuine faith will be good works.

In addition, Catholics and Protestants both say that the acts of charity born out of a genuine faith can help both individuals and the entire body of Christ to grow in righteousness and sanctification. "But speaking the truth in love, we must grow up in every way into him who is the head, into Christ, from whom the whole body, joined and knit together by every ligament with which it is equipped, as each part is working properly, promotes the body's growth in building itself up in love" (Ephesians 4:15–16).

In summary, justification is the act by which a person is regenerated and receives acquittal, forgiveness, and righteousness from God. It is also the beginning of the sanctification process. Catholics believe justification occurs initially through the sacrament of Baptism, when a person becomes a Christian either as an infant through the faith of his or her parents or as an adult through his or her personal faith. Justification can also be regained through the sacrament of Confession if it was lost due to mortal sin. Protestants believe justification occurs at the moment a person becomes a Christian by accepting Jesus as his or her Savior. Some Protestants believe justification cannot be lost, and some believe that it can be lost and regained through righting one's relationship with God, or regaining righteousness. Neither Catholics nor Protestants believe a person can grow in justification in the sense that it is the act by which God declares someone righteous, but both believe one can grow in righteousness and sanctification through acts of charity and, for Catholics, participation in the Catholic sacraments. Both Catholics and Protestants believe these acts of charity are a consequence of genuine faith and acknowledge that these works do not earn justification or salvation.

Before discussing justification within your interfaith relationship, you should each define your individual beliefs regarding justification and the terms you each use to describe this conversion.

Relationship Builders

- Both Catholics and Protestants believe justification is a free gift from God, attainable only through faith. Both also believe that justification infuses righteousness, regenerates and converts the spirit, begins the process of sanctification, and takes away sins. *Do we both believe in these principles regarding justification? Are they consistent with what we have been taught through our religious education?*

- This is a summary of the differing Catholic-Protestant beliefs regarding justification:

Catholic	Protestant
Occurs initially at baptism, when a person becomes a Christian through the faith of his/her parents. (Can also occur at the baptism of an adult through his/her personal faith.)	Occurs when a person accepts Christ and becomes a Christian.
Can occur multiple times.	Can occur multiple times. / Only occurs once.
Can be lost and regained.	Can be lost and regained. / Cannot be lost.
Does not guarantee eternal salvation.	Guarantees eternal salvation.

Do we each hold the respective Catholic and Protestant beliefs concerning justification? Why or why not?

Have our discussions through this chapter changed our individual beliefs in any way? How?

• Catholics and Protestants believe that with justification comes righteousness and sanctification, the ability to grow more Christlike through one's life. Justification can't increase or decrease; sanctification can.

What evidence do we see of the work of sanctification and God's righteousness in our lives? In our interfaith relationship?

In what ways could Christ's righteousness enrich our relationship and help our relationship to grow more Christlike?

• Catholics believe faith with works is necessary for justification and salvation in as far as the only type of genuine faith that can lead to justification and salvation is the type that will produce good works.

How has the debate of faith versus faith plus works for justification and salvation caused problems within our relationship?

Do we understand that Protestants and Catholics have essentially the same beliefs regarding this issue?

Has this understanding helped to alleviate the strain that this issue may have put on our relationship?

DIFFERENCE 6

Sacraments

"If you love me, you will keep my commandments. . . . They who have my commandments and keep them are those who love me; and those who love me will be loved by my Father, and I will love them and reveal myself to them" (John 14:15, 21).

Each of us, Catholic and Protestant alike, can probably think of an instance when a Catholic has abused a sacrament—whether it's a person who commits sins with the foreknowledge that they will be forgiven through the sacrament of Reconciliation, or the person who receives the sacrament of Holy Communion each Sunday, hung over from the night before. These types of people and their behavior give the wrong impressions of Catholics and their sacraments. Some non-Catholics see behavior such as this, which they know is not Christian behavior, and make sweeping generalizations about Catholics not being Christians, a sentiment you may have experienced firsthand in your interfaith relationship. Many also believe that Catholics view the sacraments as magical hoops to jump through for salvation, perpetuating unbiblical concepts such as earning salvation and even witchcraft.

What may surprise Catholics and Protestants, however, is that both denominations practice sacraments, although Protestants often refer to them as "ordinances." Both Catholics and Protestants recognize two sacraments, baptism and Eucharist (Lord's Supper) as actually being instituted by Christ. Catholics practice five additional sacraments—Confirmation, Reconciliation, Anointing of the Sick, Holy Orders, and Matrimony—which they too believe were established by Christ either explicitly or indirectly through his teachings. Protestants do practice some of these five as well, but generally believe that, although beneficial, they weren't instituted by Christ. Authors Geisler and MacKenzie indicate that there is no biblical or historical evidence to support that there is exactly seven sacraments, nor that the rituals other than baptism and Eucharist were intended as sacraments.[56] And, as was discussed on page 71 in *Belief 10: We Believe in the Importance of Baptism,* Protestants typically believe that sacraments are an outward sign of a person's inner sanctification, while Catholics view the sacraments as literally bestowing grace and the hope of salvation through faith.

Catholics have also been criticized because of the nature of the Catholic sacraments and the importance they place upon them. Many Protestants feel that Catholics see a sacrament in and of itself having power, saying that a ceremony alone has no power to save, and that believing actual grace flows through a sacrament "is a mystical, if not magical, view of sacraments."[57] However, it isn't the act of the sacrament that has power; without the sacrifice of Jesus and his grace within the sacrament, each would only be a meaningless ritual. Catholics do believe that Christ is the integral part of each sacrament, the sacrament only being effective because Christ himself is working through it. The actual act and administrator of each sacrament serve merely as the vehicles through which the grace of Christ is actually conferred to the participant through the power of the Holy Spirit, which, like fire, transforms all that it touches.

Each Catholic sacrament, then, consists of the actual sacramental act, the visible signs using earthy materials such as water, oil, gestures, and words. But more important, each sacrament contains the invisible power of God's grace conveyed through the Holy Spirit.

Because sacraments act through the saving power of Christ, the effectiveness of the sacrament does not depend on the spiritual state of the priest administering the sacrament. The effectiveness does, however, depend on the disposition of the recipient, or, in the case of infant baptism, the disposition of the infant's parents. The Catholic Church

---

[56]Geisler and MacKenzie, *Roman Catholics and Evangelicals,* 258–259.
[57]Ibid., 259.

teaches that both faith and reverence are absolutely necessary when receiving a sacrament. As one of Brian's former pastors once said, "Just because you sit in a garage and drink gasoline doesn't mean you are a car." The *Catechism of the Catholic Church* (1131) states: "The sacraments are efficacious signs of grace, instituted by Christ and entrusted to the Church, by which divine life is dispensed to us. The visible rites by which the sacraments are celebrated signify and make present the graces proper to each sacrament. They bear fruit in those who receive them with the required dispositions."

Another reason that Protestants generally oppose the Catholic sacraments is because teaching that God's grace—or justification—can be communicated through a sacrament disassociates a person from direct communication with God and the Holy Spirit. From a Protestant's perspective, the Catholic Church takes the place of Christ as the "one mediator between God and humankind" (1 Timothy 2:5). In addition, the Catholic perspective of sacraments gives the Catholic Church the power to control the Holy Spirit and places salvation within the control of men, not God.

But Catholics genuinely believe that God provided the seven sacraments for the enrichment and spiritual growth of Christians. Catholics attest that, while the Ten Commandments that God gave to Moses were the laws of the old covenant, the seven sacraments established by Christ are the laws, or commandments, of the new covenant. Catholics believe that they are strictly following Christ's teaching in John 14:15 (" 'If you love me, you will keep my commandments.' ") by participating in the sacraments. Anything short of not participating in the sacraments, in the eyes of a Catholic, would be to deliberately oppose the commandments of God, and "obeying the commandments of God is everything" (1 Corinthians 7:19). Not participating in the sacraments would also be shunning the gifts that God has given in the form of the sacraments. And because Catholics believe that someone who disobeyed God wouldn't be saved, the Catholic Church teaches that the sacraments are necessary for salvation. Associating the sacraments with salvation is again based upon the type of genuine faith that can lead to salvation. Catholics say that a genuine faith in Christ—the same type of faith that enables one to accept salvation—would prompt one to want to not break God's commandments, including participating in his sacraments. Therefore, participation in the sacraments is not a good work intended to save the Catholic. Rather, participation in the sacraments is a reflection of and obedience to the faith that has saved the Catholic, much as good works are a reflection of that same saving faith. (For more about good works, see *Belief 7: We Believe in Performing Good Works to Outwardly Reflect Our Inner Faith* on page 53.)

In addition, because the sacraments, based in faith, can also nourish, enrich, and express faith, Catholics view the sacraments as necessary in the process of sanctification.

Relationship Builders

- Both Catholics and Protestants practice sacraments, baptism and Eucharist being the common sacraments.
  What similarities and differences can we identify through our experiences with the sacraments of baptism and Eucharist in Protestant and Catholic churches?
  What commonalties regarding these sacraments can we use as a point of unity for our interfaith relationship?

- Protestants usually view a sacrament as being an outward sign of salvation, while Catholics believe that sanctifying grace is conferred on a recipient of a sacrament through the power of the Holy Spirit.
  What are our personal views of sacraments? Have our individual perspectives impacted our relationship in any way? How?

- The fruits of a Catholic sacrament are received only when the recipient has genuine faith.
  For the Catholic: Have I always approached a sacrament with faith, or am I guilty of thinking that I received sacramental benefits just through the ritual?

For the Protestant: Does the understanding that faith is the crux
  of every Catholic sacrament change my impression of the Catholic
  sacraments in any way?

- Protestants typically oppose the Catholic teachings of the sacra-
  ments because they believe that the sacraments wrongly place the
  Holy Spirit in the control of men.
  Because the Catholic Church has strict requirements concerning the
      administration and receiving of the sacraments, which it says are
      necessary for salvation, does either of us feel that the Catholic
      Church has too much control over salvation itself?
  How might our views impact our relationship?

DIFFERENCE 7

Catholic Sacraments Described

Therefore let us go on toward perfection, leaving behind the basic teaching about Christ, and not laying again the foundation: repentance from dead works and faith toward God, instruction about baptisms, laying on of hands, resurrection of the dead, and eternal judgment (Hebrews 6:1–2).

While the previous chapter discussed the Catholic sacraments in general, this chapter presents in detail each of the seven Catholic sacraments: Baptism, Holy Eucharist, Confirmation, Reconciliation, Anointing of the Sick, Holy Orders, and Matrimony. Also included are the biblical origins of each sacrament and why the Catholic Church believes each sacrament is so important. Protestant responses to and perspectives of the sacraments are also presented. As with other issues, strive to gain a full understanding of these sacraments so you can strengthen your interfaith relationship by identifying what beliefs you hold in common and discuss those about which you disagree.

Sacrament of Baptism

Therefore we have been buried with him by baptism into death, so that, just as Christ was raised from the dead by the glory of the Father, so we too might walk in newness of life (Romans 6:4).

Difference 7

The sacraments of Baptism, Holy Communion, and Confirmation are known as the "sacraments of initiation" because they welcome a person into the fullness of Christian life. Of these, the sacrament of baptism is considered to be the foundational sacrament. Catholics and Protestants both believe in baptism, although some disagree regarding the nature of baptism and the age at which a person should be baptized. For a thorough discussion, see *Belief 10: We Believe in the Importance of Baptism.*

Sacrament of Holy Eucharist

> Then he took a loaf of bread, and when he had given thanks, he broke it and gave it to them, saying, "This is my body, which is given for you. Do this in remembrance of me." And he did the same with the cup after supper, saying, "This cup that is poured out for you is the new covenant in my blood" (Luke 22:19–20).

Central to the practice of the Christian faith for Catholics is the sacrament of Holy Eucharist, the sacrament Catholics and Protestants both agree was instituted by Jesus at the Last Supper. Catholics take Jesus' words at the Last Supper literally (see also Matthew 26:26–28 and Mark 14:22–24) and believe that the substance of the bread and wine literally changes into the body and blood of Christ during the sacrament of Holy Eucharist, albeit the outward appearances remain the same. The process by which the bread and wine literally become the body and blood of Christ is known as "transubstantiation."

Catholics believe that this literal transformation into the body and blood of Christ is reinforced in other biblical passages. For example, John 6:54–55 contains Jesus' words to a group of skeptical Jews: " 'Those who eat my flesh and drink my blood have eternal life, and I will raise them up on the last day; for my flesh is true food and my blood is true drink.' " Catholics acknowledge that accepting the belief in transubstantiation is difficult because the transformation isn't reinforced by our senses. It is a belief that must be accepted through genuine faith.

Later in the gospel of John, Jesus says regarding this belief, " 'For this reason I have told you that no one can come to me unless it is granted by the Father' " (John 6:65). From a Catholic perspective, Jesus is saying that faith, a gift granted by his Father, is needed to accept this difficult belief. Therefore, a person without this faith wouldn't be able to accept the belief and therefore wouldn't be able to be joined with Jesus in the Eucharist and have eternal life. In this gospel, John also describes how some of Jesus' disciples left him because this teaching was difficult and offensive (John 6:66).

Transubstantiation can be compared to what happens the moment someone is baptized. When a person is baptized, there is no tangible, outward transformation; the change is all internal and invisible. God takes the person's lifeless spirit, the "bread and wine," and transforms it into a new creation. The same is true for transubstantiation—although the outward appearance of the bread and wine remain the same, in faith, the Catholic believes that their intangible qualities have changed into Christ's body and blood.

Because Catholics believe that the Eucharist bread and wine is truly Jesus, they treat these substances with reverence, a practice that has been criticized by Protestants who don't believe that Jesus is literally present in communion. Because Protestants don't believe that the communion bread is truly Jesus, some interpret the Catholic reverence for the Eucharist host as idol worship, even alleging that Catholics are worshipping demons through their communion practice.

Protestants defend their belief against transubstantiation by arguing that, although in the gospels Jesus says that this "is" his body and this "is" his blood, Jesus often spoke in figurative language—such as when he said, " 'I am the true vine, and my Father is the vinegrower' " (John 15:1)— and he is speaking figuratively here as well. Protestants acknowledge that God could work miracles, such as Catholics believe occurs in transubstantiation, but the other biblical miracles could be seen or otherwise verified, and, in their verification, give glory to God. In addition, because of the transubstantiation belief, some Protestants have accused Catholics of cannibalism, a practice obviously forbidden by the Bible.

Another objection to transubstantiation raised by Protestants is that, through transubstantiation, Christ's human body would have to be omnipresent, and Scripture only supports Christ's spiritual nature being omnipresent, such as during the Great Commission when Jesus says to his disciples, " 'I am with you always, to the end of the age' " (Matthew 28:20).

Even though they oppose the belief in transubstantiation as a whole, Protestants don't agree among themselves as to the true nature of communion. Some Protestants believe that Christ is present in communion consubstantially with the bread and wine (where Christ's body and blood exist in addition to the bread and wine), others say that he is in the communion bread and wine spiritually, while still others say that he is there symbolically.

It is also important to note that some Protestant churches have what they refer to as "open communion," in which all Christians, including Catholics, are invited to participate. Catholics, on the other hand, don't allow intercommunion with non-Catholics, in either Catholic or Protestant churches. Catholics base this practice on the teaching of Paul in 1 Corinthians 10:17: "Because there is one bread, we who are many are one body, for we all partake of the one bread." Catholics also cite 1 Corinthians 11:17–22, where Paul scolds those with divisions among them coming together to eat the Lord's supper. Because Protestants don't hold the same beliefs as Catholics regarding the substance of the Eucharist, Catholics don't believe all Christians are consuming "one bread" and don't feel they can join with other Christians in this sacrament of unity.

Another difference between Catholics and Protestants regarding Eucharist is that the sacrament of Holy Eucharist is central to the Catholic Mass and is celebrated every day of the year except for Good Friday. (See *Difference 8: Sacrifice of the Mass* starting on page 160.) Although some Protestant denominations do offer communion weekly, most Protestant churches tend to celebrate communion on a varying schedule, sometimes in preparation for holidays and sometimes monthly or at other intervals.

Sacrament of Confirmation

> *Now when the apostles at Jerusalem heard that Samaria had accepted the word of God, they sent Peter and John to them. The two went down and prayed for them that they might receive the Holy Spirit (for as yet the Spirit had not come upon any of them; they had only been baptized in the name of the Lord Jesus). Then Peter and John laid their hands on them, and they received the Holy Spirit* (Acts 8:14–17).

When an infant is baptized in the name of the Father, the Son, and the Holy Spirit, the sanctification process begins. Catholics believe that the sacrament of Confirmation is another integral step in growing in sanctification, continuing the work of the Holy Spirit that began at baptism.

Catholics believe that the sacrament of Confirmation originated from Christ's many promises to send the Holy Spirit to help continue the work he had begun, a promise fulfilled following his resurrection (John 20:22) and at Pentecost (Acts 2:1–4). As part of the Great Commission, the apostles then sought to convert people to Christ, baptizing them and enabling the Spirit to be poured upon them, as prophesied by Joel: "I will pour out my spirit on all flesh" (Joel 2:28). The apostles confirmed believers by the laying on of hands, as described in Acts 8:17: "Then Peter and John laid their hands on them, and they received the Holy Spirit." As successors to the apostles (see "Sacrament of Holy Orders" on page 155), Catholic bishops continue to carry out this commission of Jesus through the sacrament of Confirmation.

Along with the sacraments of Baptism and Holy Orders, Confirmation forever imprints on a Christian the seal of the Holy Spirit: "In him you also, when you had heard the word of truth, the gospel of your salvation, and had believed in him, were marked with the seal of the promised Holy Spirit" (Ephesians 1:13). Therefore, neither of these three sacraments can be repeated.

While Catholics see the sacrament of Confirmation marking the Christian with Christ's seal, working through the faith of the recipient,

Protestants believe they receive this mark of faith, and infusion of the Holy Spirit, through faith alone, with no sacramental influence. So while some Protestant denominations do practice confirmation, this ritual—like baptism—generally serves for Protestants as an outward sign of one's inner sanctification based on faith alone. For most Protestants, confirmation is symbolic, not actually conveying the grace of the Holy Spirit.

Sacrament of Reconciliation
(Sacrament of Penance, Confession)

> *Jesus said to them again, "Peace be with you. As the Father has sent me, so I send you." When he had said this, he breathed on them and said to them, "Receive the Holy Spirit. If you forgive the sins of any, they are forgiven them; if you retain the sins of any, they are retained"* (John 20:21–23).

The sacrament of Reconciliation is one of the two sacraments of healing because it can heal Christians of the sickness of sin. Catholics believe that Christ established this sacrament for all who have sinned but especially for those who have lost grace, justification, and the hope of salvation due to mortal sin.

Integral to understanding the sacrament of Reconciliation is knowing that the Catholic Church recognizes distinctions of sin, based on Bible passages such as 1 John 5:16–17: "If you see your brother or sister committing what is not a mortal sin, you will ask, and God will give life to such a one—to those whose sin is not mortal. There is sin that is mortal; I do not say that you should pray about that. All wrongdoing is sin, but there is sin that is not mortal." Catholics believe that mortal sins alienate a person from God. If a mortal sin is not confessed and grace received again through the sacrament of Reconciliation, that person's salvation will be in jeopardy. A sin is mortal if it is of grave matter—for example, breaking one of the Ten Commandments or one of the precepts of the Church—and if it is committed knowingly and with full consent. Venial sins, sins of less serious matter, also damage our relationship with God.

Catholics see the sacrament of Reconciliation as the means through which Jesus restores the grace of God, reinstating the justification, sanctifying grace, and hope of salvation that has been lost due to the sin. Participation in this sacrament is also encouraged for those who have committed only venial sins as the grace of God bestowed through the sacrament can assist in the growth in sanctification. In addition, confession of smaller sins through the sacrament of Reconciliation can help to prevent more serious sin because unconfessed venial sins can predispose one to commit graver sins.

Catholics and Protestants agree that the Bible commands us to forgive each other, as is stated in the "Lord's Prayer" (Matthew 6:12) and reiterated by Jesus: " 'For if you forgive others their trespasses, your heavenly Father will also forgive you' " (Matthew 6:14). But in addition, Catholics believe that Christ gave special authority, the "ministry of reconciliation," to his apostles, as described by Paul in 2 Corinthians 5:18 and 20: "All this is from God, who reconciled us to himself through Christ, and has given us the ministry of reconciliation; . . . So we are ambassadors for Christ, since God is making his appeal through us; we entreat you on behalf of Christ, be reconciled to God." As successors of the apostles (see "Sacrament of Holy Orders" on page 155), Catholic bishops and their appointees, priests, also have the apostolic authority to forgive sins through the sacrament of Reconciliation.

Most Protestants disagree with the premises behind the sacrament of Reconciliation. First, Protestants believe in confessing their sins directly to God and don't see the need to confess one's sins to another human in order to receive God's forgiveness. What some Protestants may not know, however, is that Catholics too believe in confessing their sins directly to God, outside of the confessional, and, like Protestants, believe that they are forgiven when they do so. The sacrament of Reconciliation works in conjunction with this type of confession, bestowing God's grace on those who seek to avoid mortal sin and on those whose grace has been lost due to mortal sin.

Second, Protestants do not see the sacrament of Reconciliation as being necessary for the confession of mortal sins because most believe that there are no gradations of sin, based on biblical passages such as James 2:10: "For whoever keeps the whole law but fails in one point has become accountable for all of it." Therefore, any sin, regardless of its seriousness, should be able to be confessed directly to God and be forgiven. And finally, if a Protestant believes that a saved person won't lose the promise of salvation, even due to sin, a sacrament such as this would never be needed to restore grace, justification, and ultimate salvation.

Protestants also generally disagree with the concept of "penance" that a Catholic is given by the priest after confessing sins, which usually takes the form of one or more prayers or other special deeds. Protestants often view penance as another work Catholics perform to earn salvation. Catholics maintain, however, that the purpose of the penance is to express sorrow and conversion from sin. Penance is also a consequence of a sin, the penalty for the sin that remains even after the sin has been forgiven. The penance is performed after absolution from sin (and receiving sanctifying grace) as reparation for the sins committed, not to earn or cause the absolution. (The Catholic concept of penance is related to the Catholic belief in purgatory, discussed in *Difference 9: Purgatory* beginning on page 167.)

"Those who approach the sacrament of [Reconciliation] obtain pardon from God's mercy for the offense committed against him, and are, at the same time, reconciled with the Church which they have wounded . . . (*Lumen gentium,* 11). Through the absolution of the priest and the person's faith in the redemptive power of Christ, the person is forgiven: "[W]e even boast in God through our Lord Jesus Christ, through whom we have now received reconciliation" (Romans 5:11).

Sacrament of Anointing of the Sick (Last Rites)

Are any among you sick? They should call for the elders of the church and have them pray over them, anointing them with oil in the name of the Lord. The prayer of faith will save the sick, and the Lord will raise them up; and anyone who has committed sins will be forgiven" (James 5:14–15).

The sacrament of Anointing of the Sick, or Last Rites, less commonly referred to as Extreme Unction, is the other sacrament of healing and is based upon Christ's healing of the sick and his instructions to his apostles to do the same: " 'Cure the sick' " (Matthew 10:8). As successors of the apostles (see "Sacrament of Holy Orders" on page 155), Catholic priests continue to administer this sacrament to not only those at the point of death but to any person, of any age, who is in need of physical or spiritual healing. (Because the sacrament isn't reserved for only the dying, the term "Last Rites" isn't used as frequently today as it was in the past.) This sacrament can be repeated because a person can be sick many times in his or her life, or an illness can worsen.

Some Protestants have criticized the sacrament of Anointing of the Sick, arguing that Catholics believe that without administration of this sacrament before death, they won't be saved. As was discussed in *Belief 5: We Believe in Salvation by Grace Through Faith* on page 45, however, Catholics believe that salvation is a free gift from God, one that can't be earned through works or participation in the sacraments. Catholics believe that through the sacraments, through their faith, they receive sanctifying grace to overcome sin. Through the sacrament of Anointing of the Sick, Christ's grace supports the faith of the person, strengthening the person against the propensity to sin, particularly the tendency to become discouraged and turn from God when sick or near death. Hebrews 2:14–15 describes the effect of this sacrament: "[S]o that through death he might destroy the one who has the power of death, that is, the devil, and free those who all their lives were held in slavery by the fear of death."

Most Protestants would say that a sacrament such as Anointing of the Sick isn't needed because all Christians should pray for the healing of the sick; that shouldn't just be a responsibility of the religious. Catholics support praying for the sick as well but still believe that God has a special intention for the graces available through this sacrament because it was given to the apostles by Jesus and utilizes the special authorities that Jesus gave to the apostles and to those who succeeded them.

Sacrament of Holy Orders

> And the twelve called together the whole community of the
> disciples and said, "It is not right that we should neglect the
> word of God in order to wait on tables. Therefore, friends,
> select from among yourselves seven men of good standing,
> full of the Spirit and of wisdom, whom we may appoint to
> this task." . . . They had these men stand before the apostles,
> who prayed and laid their hands on them (Acts 6:2–3, 6).

Catholics believe that the apostles, chosen by Jesus, were given special
authorities by him: "Then Jesus summoned his twelve disciples and
gave them authority over unclean spirits, to cast them out, and to cure
every disease and every sickness" (Matthew 10:1). To continue Christ's
ministry, the apostles passed their Christ-given authority onto other
selected men (see Acts 6:2–3, 6), thus instituting the sacrament of
"apostolic ministry" or Holy Orders, the Catholic sacrament of ordina-
tion. Catholic bishops and priests, therefore, have the same authorities
given to the apostles and are able to administer the sacraments instituted
by Jesus. (Catholic bishops are considered to be direct successors of the
apostles, and priests and deacons reflect those appointed by the apostles
to assist them in serving Christ's people.) Through this same apostolic
succession, Catholics believe that the pope, the leader of the Catholic
Church, is a direct successor of the leader of the apostles, Peter, and
therefore has inherited special responsibilities and authorities from
Peter. (See *Difference 10: Catholic Popes and Their Infallibility* on page
175.) In addition to being based in Scripture, apostolic succession and
the sacrament of Holy Orders are based upon the human understanding
that, since Jesus wanted his church on earth to continue, he must
provide for apostolic successors who would also need the authorities he
gave to the original apostles.

Because of the direct relationship that Catholic priests have to the
apostles and, through them, to Jesus, Catholics see the sacraments as
only being valid when administered by a Catholic priest, with the
exception of the sacrament of baptism.

In establishing requirements for the ministerial priesthood, the Catholic Church follows the example of Jesus Christ himself. First, because Jesus selected only men as his apostles, only a baptized man can be ordained in the Catholic Church. Second, Catholic priests are expected to remain celibate. Through celibacy, priests believe that they are obeying Jesus' words regarding personal sacrifice in Matthew 19:29. Celibacy also allows priests to give their undivided attention to the affairs of Christ and the Church, as Paul advises in 1 Corinthians 7:32–34: "I want you to be free from anxieties. The unmarried man is anxious about the affairs of the Lord, how to please the Lord; but the married man is anxious about the affairs of the world, how to please his wife, and his interests are divided."

Because the sacrament of Holy Orders confers a permanent spiritual mark on the soul, like the sacraments of Baptism and Confirmation, it cannot be repeated.

Protestant churches ordain their church leaders as well, although most don't recognize the rite as a sacrament. In Protestant churches, as in Catholic churches, leaders are ordained by the laying on of hands by the church elders. Most Protestant pastors are married, recognizing that marriage was established and encouraged by God in the beginning and acknowledging that the Bible doesn't forbid people of God to marry. In fact, in 1 Timothy 3:1–13, Paul describes the qualities that bishops and deacons of the church should possess, including being married no more than once. For even though Paul says in 1 Corinthians 7:7, "I wish that all were as I myself am," i.e., unmarried, he recognizes that "each has a particular gift from God, one having one kind and another a different kind."

Furthermore, because the Bible indicates in some passages that women can be church leaders (see 1 Timothy 3:11), some Protestant churches have ordained women as ministers.

Protestants typically don't support the Catholic Church's claim to apostolic succession. Protestants also don't accept the inherent apostolic authorities of the Catholic popes, bishops, and priests, saying that no biblical evidence indicates that the authorities of any of the apostles were to be transferred. Some Protestants point out that the definition of apostle is one who has seen Christ firsthand (1 Corinthians 9:1) and has been given authorities to perform "the signs of a true apostle" (2 Corinthians 12:12). Because no one other than those who were first-hand witnesses of Christ can be apostles, true apostolic succession and apostolic authority as described by the Catholic Church cannot exist.[58]

Sacrament of Matrimony

> *Some Pharisees came to him, and to test him they asked, "Is it lawful for a man to divorce his wife for any cause?" He answered, "Have you not read that the one who made them at the beginning 'made them male and female,' and said, 'For this reason a man shall leave his father and mother and be joined to his wife, and the two shall become one flesh'? So they are no longer two, but one flesh. Therefore what God has joined together, let no one separate"* (Matthew 19:3–6).

Marriage has existed in the world since the beginning, when God created Eve for Adam, saying, " 'It is not good that the man should be alone' " (Genesis 2:18). Catholics believe that Jesus elevated marriage to a sacramental level in passages such as that above, where he "invests it with a new grace and power which existed only 'in the beginning,' when God directly gave this grace of fidelity to Adam and Eve before their sin."[59]

In addition, Catholics believe that the sacrament of marriage symbolizes Christ's unity with his church, described by Paul in Ephesians 5:31–32: " 'For this reason a man will leave his father and mother and be joined to his wife, and the two will become one flesh.' This is a great mystery, and I am applying it to Christ and the church." (See also Ephesians 5:21–33.) The marriage covenant made between a man and a woman in marriage, uniting the man and woman with each other and with God, is modeled upon the new covenant made between Christ and the church.

[58]Ibid., 211.

[59]Schreck, *Catholic and Christian,* 149.

Although Protestants don't normally recognize marriage as a sacrament, Catholics and Protestants agree on the nature of marriage. Through the covenant of marriage, the husband and wife strive not only for one flesh but also for one heart and soul. It is through marriage that couples also fulfill God's command to " 'be fruitful and multiply' " (Genesis 1:28). And while marriage reflects Christ's union with the church, it also mirrors the exclusive, faithful relationship a Christian must have with his God.

Because marriage is a covenant freely made between a man, a woman, and God, it is indissoluble. Jesus himself condemned divorce, saying, " 'Whoever divorces his wife, except for unchastity, and marries another commits adultery' " (Matthew 19:9). Therefore, a Catholic who divorces cannot be married again in the Catholic Church unless an annulment is granted. An annulment may be granted if one or both of the partners didn't give free consent, wasn't capable of giving free consent, or wasn't open to the possibility of children.[60] Because the annulment option is only used to recognize an invalid marriage, it is not considered to be a fail-safe for Catholics who enter into marriage willingly, nor will it be granted to those who have enough money to pay for it, as is sometimes thought. A Catholic whose spouse has died can be remarried in the Catholic Church, because the couple kept their vow to be together until death.

On the other hand, Protestants do not practice any form of annulment. And although Protestants do not encourage divorce, most churches will remarry people who have been divorced.

Relationship Builders

* Although based in Catholic Church teachings and traditions, the seven Catholic sacraments are also biblically grounded, Catholics say.
  How does each of us feel about the biblical basis for each of the Catholic sacraments?

---

[60]R. Lawler, Wuerl, and T. C. Lawler, *Teaching of Christ,* 512.

Difference 7

Do these roots provide enough "proof" for either of us to validate the Catholic Church teachings about the sacraments?
In what ways has the issue of the Catholic sacraments impacted our interfaith relationship?

* This chapter explains the seven Catholic sacraments:

   Baptism

   Holy Eucharist

   Confirmation

   Reconciliation

   Anointing of the Sick

   Holy Orders

   Matrimony

   What are our impressions of each of these sacraments?
   Have our perceptions changed after learning more about the details of each sacrament. How?
   Has our increased understanding helped to resolve any problems within our interfaith relationship?

DIFFERENCE 8

Sacrifice of the Mass

For I received from the Lord what I also handed on to you, that the Lord Jesus on the night when he was betrayed took a loaf of bread, and when he had given thanks, he broke it and said, "This is my body that is for you. Do this in remembrance of me." In the same way he took the cup also, after supper, saying, "This cup is the new covenant in my blood. Do this, as often as you drink it, in remembrance of me." For as often as you eat this bread and drink the cup, you proclaim the Lord's death until he comes (1 Corinthians 11:23–26).

Both Catholics and Protestants participate in worship services traditionally on Sunday (see *Belief 15: We Believe in Respecting the Sabbath* on page 97), and both practice the sacrament of Holy Eucharist at these services (see *Difference 6: Sacraments* on page 141). However, unlike most Protestant services, the Catholic worship service, the "Mass"—which comes from the Latin word *missa* in the Latin dismissal for the service, "*Ite missa est*," meaning, "Go, it is ended"[61]—is intrinsic with the celebration of the sacrament of Holy Eucharist, so much so that the Mass itself is considered a sacrament. The *Catechism* explains that "the Mass is at the same time, and inseparably, the sacrificial memorial in which the sacrifice of the cross is perpetuated and the sacred banquet of communion with the Lord's body and blood."[62] The Catholic use of "sacrifice" to describe the Mass is controversial because most Protestants believe this concept goes against the biblical teachings

---

[61]*The Maryknoll Catholic Dictionary,* ed. Albert J. Nevins (Wilkes-Barre, Pa.: Dimension Books, 1965), 361.

[62]*CCC*, 1382.

of Christ's one sacrifice, such as Hebrews 9:25, which explicitly says that Christ won't "offer himself again and again."

Catholics and Protestants both believe that Christ's one sacrifice was sufficient for salvation; re-sacrifice is unnecessary, as well as unbiblical. And re-sacrificing Christ, Catholics and Protestants agree, is clearly against Scripture, which states that Christ was sacrificed one time only, something never to be repeated. In Romans 6:10, Paul says that "the death he died, he died to sin, once for all." And the author of Hebrews 10:12 says, "Christ had offered for all time a single sacrifice for sins." Therefore, much of the controversy concerning the Mass as a sacrifice may well be summarized in these questions: Can Christ's sacrifice, completed on Calvary "once for all" (Romans 6:10), be re-presented or memorialized without denouncing the atonement provided for in the original sacrifice? Catholics say yes; Protestants say no. And is a re-presentation of Christ's sacrifice in the Mass biblically based and even necessary? Again, Catholics say yes; Protestants say no.

Why do Catholics believe so strongly that the sacrifice of the Mass is required by Christ, its roots being strongly anchored in the Bible, and that the Mass is only a memorial of Christ's original sacrifice? Understanding clearly the crux or focal point of the Mass, the sacrament of Holy Eucharist, may help to clarify the Catholic perspectives.

The practice of the Catholic Mass is based first upon Jesus' institution of the sacrament of Holy Eucharist at the Last Supper. As was discussed in the "Sacrament of Holy Eucharist" section of *Difference 7: Catholic Sacraments Described* on page 146, Catholics believe in transubstantiation; that is, they believe that, at the Last Supper, Jesus literally changed bread and wine into his body and blood, a miracle that continues to this day through the sacrament of Holy Eucharist. And as was presented in the "Sacrament of Holy Orders" on page 155 of this same chapter, Catholics believe that only Catholic bishops and priests, because of their direct connection with the original apostles, are authorized by Christ to preside over both the sacrament of Holy Eucharist and the Mass.

Catholics believe that at the Last Supper, Jesus not only instituted the sacrament of Holy Eucharist but also commanded that the apostles continue meeting for these fellowship meals, the first Catholic Masses, when he said, " 'Do this in remembrance of me' " (Luke 22:19; see also 1 Corinthians 11:24). Paul corroborates Christ's command in 1 Corinthians 11:26: "For as often as you eat this bread and drink the cup, you proclaim the Lord's death until he comes." Catholics believe that Jesus wanted to leave his followers "a visible sacrifice (as the nature of man demands) by which the bloody sacrifice which he was to accomplish once for all on the cross would be re-presented, its memory perpetuated until the end of the world, and its salutary power be applied to the forgiveness of the sins we daily commit."[63]

The Catholic Mass, then, is a re-presentation of Christ's one and only sacrifice. Because Jesus is "the same yesterday and today and forever" (Hebrews 13:8) and "holds his priesthood permanently" (Hebrews 7:24), Catholics don't believe that Christ is re-sacrificed during each Mass but that God makes the same Jesus who suffered in the past again literally present during the sacrament of Holy Eucharist.

Looking into the Mass more deeply, Catholics—and Protestants— view Christ as the sacrificial lamb who " 'was slaughtered to receive power and wealth and wisdom and might and honor and glory and blessing' " (Revelation 5:12). Catholics believe that the Christ who was sacrificed for the sin of the world is really and truly present in the Eucharist through the sacrament of Holy Eucharist. Therefore, coexistent with Christ's body and blood in the Eucharist is the salvation he purchased with that same body and blood, which is why Christ says, " 'Those who eat my flesh and drink my blood have eternal life, and I will raise them up on the last day' " (John 6:54). In the sacrifice of the Mass, then, Catholics remember Christ's sacrifice of body and blood—presently contained in the Eucharist—by freely offering back to God and glorifying him with the gifts in the Eucharist that he has given us, "so that God may be glorified in all things through

---

[63]*CCC*, 1366, quoting Council of Trent (1562): Denzinger-Schonmetzer 1740.

Jesus Christ" (1 Peter 4:11), thus giving the sacrificial dimension to the Mass.

Therefore, Catholics do consider the Eucharist to be a sacrifice that re-presents, or makes present again, Christ's sacrifice, because it memorializes Christ's one sacrifice, and because it applies the fruits of that sacrifice.

Because Catholics believe that Christ is truly present at the Catholic Mass through the sacrament of Holy Eucharist, they also believe that a person can receive certain fruits, or benefits, from attending Mass and participating in the sacrament of Holy Eucharist, including growing closer to Christ, to the Church, and to other Christians, and receiving forgiveness of venial sins and preservation from mortal sins. As with participation in the Catholic sacraments, participation in the Mass can help the Catholic to grow in sanctification. But it must also be mentioned that, as in the case of all Catholic sacraments, a person must approach the Mass and the sacrament of Holy Eucharist with genuine faith and with the proper disposition. Without faith and the proper reverence toward God, the Mass becomes ritualistic. (Catholics believe that another benefit that can come out of the Mass, considered in itself to be a prayer in which God is glorified, is help for souls in purgatory. The belief in purgatory brings strong opposition from Protestants and is discussed in *Difference 9: Purgatory* starting on page 167.)

Most Protestants disagree with Catholic concept of the Mass as a sacrifice. Geisler and MacKenzie say that, through his command to " 'do this in remembrance of me,' " Jesus meant for believers to participate in communion to remember his sacrifice on the cross, not to reenact it.[64] And even though the Catholic Church claims it is memorializing Christ's one sacrifice, some Protestants still feel that Catholics aren't merely re-presenting Christ's one sacrifice but are literally sacrificing him over and over again. But even those Protestants who accept that Catholics are only re-presenting Christ's one sacrifice disagree with the practice. Geisler and MacKenzie write: "The whole concept of re-enacting and re-presenting Christ's sacrifice on the cross

---

[64]Geisler and MacKenzie, *Roman Catholics and Evangelicals,* 267.

is contrary to the clear teaching of Hebrews that this sacrifice occurred once for all time."[65] Other Protestants say that the idea of Christ's sacrifice even being re-presented at the Mass detracts from Christ's one atonement for all sins. Protestants also question why a representation of the sacrifice would even be needed in light of Jesus' words right before his death: " 'It is finished' " (John 19:30).

In addition, because the Mass recreates the sacrifice of Christ, many Protestants view the Mass as being a reminder of sins and guilt that must be atoned for over and over. They see the Catholic Mass as being based upon Old Testament sacrifices, where "there is a reminder of sin year after year" (Hebrews 10:3). Referring to Old Testament sacrifices, author Dave Hunt says, "The repetition of those offerings is given as proof that they could not pay the penalty for sin; and the fact that Christ was offered only once is given as proof that His sacrifice was sufficient and never needed to be repeated. That the Mass must be repeated proves its ineffectiveness."[66] Recreating Christ's sacrifice seems to some Protestants to invalidate Scripture like Hebrews 9:28, which says that Christ was "offered once to bear the sins of many," and Hebrews 10:14, which says, "For by a single offering he has perfected for all time those who are sanctified." Further, most Protestants agree with Lutzer: "The priesthood, the perpetual nature of the offerings, the perception that salvation is unfinished—all of this fails to appreciate the radical difference the coming of Christ made."[67]

Another controversy that sometimes arises between Catholics and Protestants related to the sacrifice of the Mass is the Catholic use of the crucifix, where the sacrificed Christ is represented on the cross. As with the sacrifice of the Mass, many Protestants think that the use of the crucifix perpetuates Christ's sacrifice, fixating on the crucified Christ rather than on the risen Lord.

In spite of Protestant oppositions, Catholics hold that the Mass is required by God. In *The Lamb's Supper,* author Dr. Scott Hahn describes

---

[65]Ibid.

[66]Dave Hunt, *A Woman Rides the Beast* (Eugene, Oreg.: Harvest House Publishers, 1994), 370–371.

[67]Lutzer, *Doctrines That Divide,* 109.

how the Catholic Mass is a perpetual renewal of the new covenant, God having established programs of renewal for all of the covenants he made.[68] Because attending Mass is considered to be a renewal of the new covenant and participating in the Catholic sacraments, including the sacrament of Holy Communion, is considered to be obeying the laws of the new covenant, the Catholic Church requires its members to attend Mass on Sundays and on the six holy days of obligation, "the appointed festivals of the Lord our God" (2 Chronicles 2:4):

Christmas: December 25

Solemnity of Mary: January 1

Jesus' Ascension: forty days after Easter

Assumption of Mary: August 15

All Saints' Day: November 1

Immaculate Conception: December 8

Mass attendance is not an act or a good work designed to earn salvation. Rather, like participation in all of the Catholic sacraments, it is an expression of the *faith* of the Catholic similar to obeying the commands of Christ and accepting his grace. The Catholic should want to attend Mass regularly to participate in the renewal of the new covenant established by Christ.

Relationship Builders

• Catholics and Protestants agree that Christ only needed to sacrifice himself once.
  Do we believe as a Catholic and as a Protestant in the sufficiency of Christ's one sacrifice?

• Catholics believe that the same Christ who was sacrificed only once is made present again through the sacrament of Holy Eucharist.
  What do each of us believe is the essence of the sacrament of Holy Eucharist?

---

[68]Scott Hahn, *The Lamb's Supper: The Mass as Heaven on Earth* (New York: Doubleday, 1999), 157–158.

> *Do we believe that Christ is truly present in the sacrament or is this a doctrine that has caused problems within our interfaith relationship?*

- Many Protestants hold that Catholics are sacrificing Christ over and over at the Mass. Other Protestants question why even a reenactment of Christ's one sacrifice is necessary.

  Does either of us feel that Christ is being resacrificed through the Catholic Mass? Why or why not?

- The Catholic Church requires Mass attendance on Sundays and holy days of obligation.

  Do we both agree that the Catholic Church should mandate Mass attendance on Sundays? What about on holy days?

  How has this requirement affected our interfaith relationship?

  Has it made it difficult to incorporate Protestant worship into our faith practice as a couple?

DIFFERENCE 9

Purgatory

But nothing unclean will enter [heaven], nor anyone who practices abomination or falsehood, but only those who are written in the Lamb's book of life (Revelation 21:27).

As was discussed in *Belief 9: We Believe in the Reality of Sin and the Forgiveness of Sins* beginning on page 65, Christ's death paid the price for our sins. Suffering and dying on the cross at Calvary, he satisfied God's law by absorbing God's wrath for every sin that was committed and would ever be committed. But the Bible gives definite examples that, even after sins have been forgiven, punishments and repercussions for sins remain. For example, believers, though their sins are forgiven through Christ's sacrifice, still suffer the same consequences for Adam and Eve's original sin as every other person, namely, painful childbirth, the need to labor, and death. Another example of a penalty for sin that had to be paid after the sin was forgiven is recorded in 2 Samuel 12:13–14. In this passage, after David had sinned through adultery with Bathsheba, "David said to Nathan, 'I have sinned against the Lord.' Nathan said to David, 'Now the Lord has put away your sin; you shall not die. Nevertheless, because by this deed you have utterly scorned the Lord, the child that is born to you shall die.' "

The Catholic doctrine of purgatory is based upon the concept of offering reparation for sins committed, even those sins that have been forgiven. Purgatory is the way in which Catholics believe that the penalties for forgiven sins, and unconfessed venial sins, are paid through suffering after death, purifying the person because no one with even a stain from sin can enter heaven. (Catholics believe that, while a person who dies with venial sins will enter purgatory, a person who dies in a state of mortal sin will go to eternal hell. See "Sacrament of Reconciliation" in *Difference 7: Catholic Sacraments Described* on page 151 for more about mortal and venial sins.)

It is not known whether purgatory is a place, a process, or a state of being. It is also not known what form of punishment or purification may occur there. Some believe that purgatory includes both positive punishment along with pain from being in the absence of God. What the Catholic Church teaches about purgatory is this: "All who die in God's grace and friendship, but still imperfectly purified, are indeed assured of their eternal salvation; but after death they undergo purification, so as to achieve the holiness necessary to enter the joy of heaven."[69]

Contrary to some opinions, purification in purgatory is not a work intended to earn a person's admission to heaven. It is a purification process through suffering over which the person has no control—just as one cannot control suffering on earth, nor control penalties for sins such as painful childbirth, one cannot control the suffering in purgatory. It is something that is endured. Neither is purgatory a form of vengeance from God—God's vengeance was atoned for by Christ. The penalties of purgatory follow from the very nature of sin, adhering to the punishment God's law allows for sins, even forgiven sins. (The penance that a person is asked to say following the absolution from and forgiveness of sins in the sacrament of Reconciliation is similar in concept to purgatory. The person's sins have been forgiven, yet reparation must still be made. See "Sacrament of Reconciliation" in *Difference 7: Catholic Sacraments Described* on page 151.)

Catholics believe that in purgatory, a soul will be cleansed similarly to how Isaiah's lips were purified with fire before he began his prophetic ministry for the Lord: " 'Now that this has touched your lips, your guilt has departed and your sin is blotted out' " (Isaiah 6:7). Catholics also interpret Paul's teaching in 1 Corinthians 3:10–15, where Paul says how our works will be tested, as describing the purification role of a place like purgatory: "If what has been built on the foundation

---

[69]*CCC,* 1030.

survives," Paul says, "the builder will receive a reward . . . [But] if the work is burned up, the builder will suffer loss; the builder will be saved, but only as through fire" (1 Corinthians 3:14–15). In purgatory, the soul would suffer the temporary loss of God as it is purified through the fire of punishment and suffering in order to eventually live in God's presence eternally.

Other biblical passages seem to support the existence of a place separate from heaven and hell, which could be a purgatory. In Psalm 139:8, David describes how God is everywhere, from the heavens to the nether world. "Nether world" couldn't refer to the hell of eternal damnation because we know that God isn't present in that hell based on 2 Thessalonians 1:9: "These will suffer the punishment of eternal destruction, separated from the presence of the Lord and from the glory of his might." Could David have been referring to a purgatory? In Matthew 12:32, Jesus describes how blasphemy against the Spirit will not be forgiven " 'either in this age or in the age to come,' " implying that, although the sin described by Jesus is unforgivable, forgiveness of other sins could occur in the next life, perhaps in purgatory.

More biblical passages that could support purgatory include Hebrews 12:23, which refers to the "spirits of the righteous made perfect," possibly describing the purification of souls in purgatory. In 1 Peter 3:19–20, Peter describes that, after Christ died, "he went and made a proclamation to the spirits in prison, who in former times did not obey." Perhaps this "prison" was purgatory. And Revelation 20:13 describes the judgment of the dead: "And the sea gave up the dead that were in it, Death and Hades gave up the dead that were in them, and all were judged according to what they had done." This passage lists multiple places, other than heaven, where the dead could be. The next verse, "Then Death and Hades were thrown into the lake of fire" (Revelation 20:14), could mean that Death—the state defeated by Christ—and Hades—which could be purgatory—were destroyed in the eternal hell.

But perhaps one of the most convincing Catholic arguments for the existence of purgatory comes in 2 Maccabees 12:44–45, describing the actions of Judas Maccabeus, the commander of the Jewish troops, following a battle:

> For if he were not expecting that those who had fallen would rise again, it would have been superfluous and foolish to pray for the dead. But if he was looking to the splendid reward that is laid up for those who fall asleep in godliness, it was a holy and pious thought. Therefore he made atonement for the dead, so that they might be delivered from their sin.

In this passage, Maccabeus describes how he prays for the dead. Catholics argue that souls in heaven wouldn't need prayers, and souls in hell wouldn't be helped by prayers. Therefore, based on this passage, souls must exist in some other place where their suffering can be helped by prayers of those on earth, that place being purgatory. For Protestants, the trouble with using the Maccabees passage in support of purgatory is that it falls within the deuterocanonical books, or the Apocrypha, those disputed books that are contained in the Catholic Bible but not in the Protestant Bible, and therefore have no theological authority for Protestants. (See *Difference 11: Accepted "Inspired" Books of the Bible* on page 183.)

Praying for the dead, as described in the Maccabees passage, is a Catholic practice that is tied to the doctrine of purgatory. Just as all Christians believe that intercessory prayers can help those suffering on earth, Catholics believe that prayers they say for the dead—those in purgatory, because those in hell are already eternally damned—can help persuade God to have mercy on their souls and ease their suffering. Catholic Masses are often said for people who have died as a form of intercessory prayer for comfort and alleviation of their suffering.

Indulgences are also related to prayers for the dead and offering reparations for sins in purgatory, "based on the principle that every prayer, good work, or penance offered to God in faith for the remission of the effects of sin is effective."[70] An indulgence is a remission of punishment due to forgiven sins. Indulgences, which can be applied for

---

[70]Schreck, *Essential Catholic Catechism*, 388.

the living or the dead, can be obtained through prayers and other activities and can be part of one's atonement, or penance, for one's own sins or the sins of another in purgatory. Indulgences are considered either partial or plenary, removing either some or all of the temporal punishment due to sin. An indulgence can be substituted for the reparation for sins that would normally have been offered over that period. After Nathan informed David that his child would die as a penalty for his sin, David "therefore pleaded with God for the child; David fasted, and went in and lay all night on the ground" (2 Samuel 12:16). Through his actions, David was appealing to God's mercy for reprieve from the punishment for his forgiven sin; his appeal was a form of indulgence. And Job himself offered sacrifices for his children after their feast days, hoping to appease God if " 'my children have sinned, and cursed God in their hearts' " (Job 1:5). Through his sacrifices, Job was appealing for an indulgence from God for the penalties of sin his children might have to pay. Like praying for mercy and reprieve for suffering on this earth, indulgences offer reprieve for suffering in purgatory.

Indulgences were the primary impetus for the Protestant Reformation because Luther vehemently opposed the selling of them, an abusive practice in his day that is no longer supported by the Catholic Church. Luther didn't initially oppose the doctrine of purgatory but later rejected it because of its connection with indulgences.[71] (And, Catholics argue, Luther supported the canon that didn't include the Maccabees books because they supported purgatory and contradicted his concept of justification by faith alone. See *Difference 11: Accepted "Inspired" Books of the Bible* on page 183.)

Most Protestants today agree with Luther and reject the doctrine of purgatory, saying that the biblical evidence for it is weak and ambiguous and that it is based primarily on tradition and human speculation. Some Protestants believe that a person is saved and the soul wiped clean of sin once and for all time when he or she accepts Christ. This promise of salvation cannot be lost, regardless of any sin that the person commits,

---

[71]Geisler and MacKenzie, *Roman Catholics and Evangelicals,* 331, 222.

so admission to heaven is assured and a place like purgatory is not needed and therefore nonexistent.

Protestants who believe that the assurance of their salvation can be lost and regained also usually don't accept the idea of purgatory, believing that a person must just confess sins in order to regain a right standing with God. Furthermore, many Protestants say that the doctrine of purgatory undermines the sufficiency of Christ's work on the cross. Right before Jesus died, he said, " 'It is finished' " (John 19:30). If more purification were to exist in a purgatory, Protestants argue, Christ wouldn't have been able to make this statement. Furthermore, in Galatians 3:13, Paul says, "Christ redeemed us from the curse of the law by becoming a curse for us," which some Protestants interpret as meaning that Christ's sacrifice took away not only sins themselves but also all reparation that may ever have had to be offered for the sins.

Purgatory also contradicts the concept that upon death, a person will go to only one of two places: heaven and hell, a belief supported by biblical passages such as Luke 23:43, when Jesus said to the criminal being crucified with him, " 'Truly I tell you, today you will be with me in Paradise.' " Even though Christ may have forgiven the man's sins, shouldn't the criminal still have had to make reparation for the sins in purgatory?

More biblical passages exist that seem to question the existence of purgatory. Hebrews 10:1–18 describes the sufficiency of Christ's one sacrifice and the establishment of the new covenant, concluding with: "[The Lord] also adds, 'I will remember their sins and their lawless deeds no more.' Where there is forgiveness of these, there is no longer any offering for sin" (Hebrews 10:17–18), which would include sin offerings in purgatory. Psalm 130:3 says, "If you, O Lord, should mark iniquities, Lord, who could stand?" Would the God described in this passage keep track of sins for which reparation must be given in purgatory? And Psalm 32 speaks of the joy of forgiveness, opening with: "Happy are those whose transgression is forgiven, whose sin is covered. Happy are those to whom the Lord imputes no iniquity, and in whose spirit there is no deceit" (Psalm 32:1–2). This passage seems to say that not only will people's sins not be held against them but also that no reparation for sins, on earth or in purgatory, will be required.

Protestants also reject the Catholic concept of indulgences, believing that because a Catholic must perform good works or actions to receive them, indulgences are another way in which Catholics think they can earn salvation. But Catholics genuinely believe that they cannot earn salvation and that through their actions, they are only doing what is required by God's law, living out their faith, in the case of good works, and offering reparation for sins, in the case of indulgences.

Purgatory is another doctrinal belief for which no clear biblical evidence exists to confirm or deny its existence. My father-in-law, who was raised Catholic and is now a Protestant pastor, says his view is that he knows if he has accepted Christ, then he will be received into heaven. Whether the route he will take to get there is a direct one or will include a detour through a place like purgatory is something that neither he nor anyone else knows. Like him, you need to focus on the point that, as Christians, you will be saved, regardless of the existence of purgatory. And as with the other disputed Catholic-Protestant beliefs, strive to understand the issue from both Catholic and Protestant perspectives. Talk about any insights that you may have and how the existence or nonexistence of purgatory may impact your interfaith relationship.

Relationship Builders

- Even after God has forgiven a sin, a person may have to suffer repercussions for the sin.
  What problems can we identify in today's world that may be repercussions for committed sins?
  Can we see any repercussions for sins affecting our own lives?
  How could the repercussions from these sins be affecting our interfaith relationship?

- Purgatory is the place or process through which Catholics believe that Christians make reparation for forgiven sins or unconfessed venial sins.

How do we each feel about the existence of purgatory?
Even though we may not agree on this doctrine, do we understand
that we can be saved with or without accepting this belief?

* Biblical evidence exists that could support a belief in a place like
purgatory.
Is the biblical evidence supporting the existence of purgatory
convincing enough for either of us? Why or why not?
How do we feel about the support for purgatory in 2 Maccabees,
being that this book is part of the Catholic Bible and not part of
the Protestant Bible?

* Most Protestants don't accept the doctrine of purgatory, believing
that biblical evidence for it is weak and that it detracts from the
saving work of Christ.
The Protestant unbelief in purgatory may eliminate guilt from past
sins for which a Catholic still feels he or she must offer reparation
in purgatory. Could guilt from past sins—perhaps perpetuated by
the Catholic doctrine of purgatory—be adding an unnecessary
burden to our interfaith relationship?
What are some steps we could take as a couple to unleash this
burden?

DIFFERENCE 10

Catholic Popes and Their Infallibility

[Jesus said,] "And I tell you, you are Peter, and on this rock I will build my church, and the gates of Hades will not prevail against it. I will give you the keys of the kingdom of heaven, and whatever you bind on earth will be bound in heaven, and whatever you loose on earth will be loosed in heaven" (Matthew 16:18–19).

When Christ established his church here on earth, Christians believe that Christ intended his church to be "the church of the living God" (1 Timothy 3:15), "devoted . . . to the apostles' teaching" (Acts 2:42) and led by the "Spirit of truth" (John 16:13). For reasons presented in the "Sacrament of Holy Orders" portion of *Difference 7: Catholic Sacraments Described* on page 155, Catholics believe that Catholic bishops are direct successors of the apostles, and Catholic priests reflect those appointed by the apostles to spread the gospel of Christ. Catholics also believe that Jesus singled out the apostle Peter as the first leader of the church, and the special authorities given to him—including his controversial infallibility—have been passed onto his successors, the Catholic popes.

As was also discussed previously, Protestants disagree with apostolic succession. In addition, both Peter's position as the first pope and the infallibility of the pope have been questioned and disputed by Protestants.

175

The Catholic belief in Peter as the first pope is based both in Scripture and in tradition. Catholics believe that when Christ first met the apostle Peter, known then as Simon, he immediately selected him as the leader of his church on earth. At this first meeting, Jesus says to Simon, " 'You are Simon son of John. You are to be called Cephas' (which is translated Peter)" (John 1:42), meaning "rock." Catholics point out that Christ didn't do meaningless gestures and believe that Jesus deliberately changed Simon's name to Peter as a precursor of the future plans he had for him.

Later, in Matthew 16:18–19, Catholics believe that Jesus officially appoints Peter as the first leader of the church, saying that Peter is the rock upon which he will build his church (Matthew 16:18). Jesus also presents Peter with the special authorities he will need in this position, giving him the "keys of the kingdom of heaven" and telling him that " 'whatever you bind on earth will be bound in heaven, and whatever you loose on earth will be loosed in heaven' " (Matthew 16:19). A similar authority to bind and loose is later given to the other apostles (Matthew 18:18), but here this authority is given uniquely to Peter.

Catholics also cite further biblical evidence that Jesus appointed Peter as the head of the church. Peter is most often named first when the names of the apostles are listed in Scripture (Matthew 10:2, Mark 3:16, Luke 6:14, and Acts 1:13), and he is the one who often speaks for the apostles (Matthew 18:21, Luke 12:41, John 6:68–69). Also, Peter is named 191 times in the New Testament, where the names of the other apostles combined are mentioned about 130 times.[72] In addition, Catholics believe that Jesus reiterates Peter's position as leader of the church when, following his resurrection, Jesus tells Peter to " 'feed my lambs, . . . tend my sheep, . . . feed my sheep, . . . [and] follow me' " (John 21:15, 16, 17, 19).

Catholics say that history also supports Peter's position of leadership and the passing of his leadership authorities to his successors. A strong Christian tradition says that the apostles Peter and Paul both were martyred in Rome and that the bishop of Rome was in time considered

---

[72]Frank Chacon and Jim Burnham, *Beginning Apologetics 1, How to Explain and Defend the Catholic Faith* (Farmington, N. Mex.: San Juan Catholic Seminars, 1998), 15.

to be the apostolic successor of Peter and Paul collectively.[73] The bishop of Rome eventually came to be thought of as the successor of the apostle Peter only based on study of the biblical passages cited earlier and the teachings based on these passages by prominent church leaders.

The infallibility of the pope is also a doctrine that has been debated by Catholics and Protestants. The pope's infallibility is based in the infallibility that Catholics believe Christ promised to his church. In John 16:13, Jesus says, " 'When the Spirit of truth comes, he will guide you into all the truth; for he will not speak on his own, but will speak whatever he hears, and he will declare to you the things that are to come.' " Based on Jesus' promise, the Catholic Church believes that when the church leaders, the council of bishops, come together—as the council at Jerusalem did in Acts 15—and invoke the help of the Holy Spirit, they cannot as a group be wrong upon a matter of Christian faith upon which they agree. The ability to make error-free doctrinal decisions under the guidance of the Holy Spirit is what the Catholic Church defines as the gift of infallibility.

And just as Jesus gave authorities to Peter that were similar to yet separate from those authorities given to the other apostles, the Catholic Church also believes that God gave Peter—and his successors—the gift of infallibility that he gave to the apostles as a group and their successors as a group. This belief in the pope's infallibility is rooted in Scripture but is also based on traditional beliefs of the church and was only formally defined by the First Vatican Council of 1869–70.

Catholics base their belief in the pope's infallibility on instances in Scripture when Peter received individual inspirations from the Holy Spirit, including when Peter was moved to describe Jesus as the Son of God (Matthew 16:13–17) and when Peter was led by the Spirit to baptize the Gentiles (Acts 10). In Luke 22:31–32, Jesus also prays for the strength of Peter's faith, which Catholics see as supporting the gift of infallibility and leadership position that God intends for Peter and his successors: " 'Simon, Simon, listen! Satan has demanded to sift all of you like wheat, but I have prayed for you that your own faith may not

---

[73]Schreck, *Catholic and Christian,* 88.

fail; and you, when once you have turned back, strengthen your brothers.' "

What neither Catholics nor Protestants may realize, however, is that the pope's infallibility as is taught by the Catholic Church is extremely limited. Not everything the pope says nor everything he teaches is infallible. As a human, the pope can make the same errors in his teachings as any other person. A pope's statement can only be considered infallible if it meets these conditions:

1. The pope must be speaking *ex cathedra,* that is, "from the chair" of Peter, which means in his position as chief teacher and shepherd of Catholic Christians.

2. The pope must clearly define the doctrine as being a truth of faith.

3. It must be a definition concerning "faith or morals."[74]

That being said, the pope has made only two infallible declarations in recent times: the Immaculate Conception of Mary (1854) and Mary's assumption into heaven (1950) because these were issues about which some Catholics had questions. When the pope speaks or writes something about a topic outside of these criteria, this teaching should be valued for its content but is not considered to be an infallible teaching.

Protestants as a whole disagree that Peter was the first pope and also disregard the doctrine of papal infallibility. Protestants say that there is no biblical evidence of the establishment of the papacy nor that Peter gained any kind of supremacy in New Testament times. Referring to the passage where Jesus said, " 'You are Peter, and on this rock I will build my church' " (Matthew 16:18), Protestants argue that "rock" refers to Peter's prior proclamation that Jesus is Lord, Jesus being the "rock" upon which the church will be built. In support of this view, Protestants point out that Jesus refers to Peter consistently in the second person ("you") in this conversation and therefore should have used "you" again instead of "this rock" if he were indeed referring to Peter.

---

[74]Schreck, *Catholic and Christian,* 96, partially quoting First Vatican Council, Pastor Aeternus, chap. 4, in *Documents of Vatican I,* 63.

Protestants also note that in Greek, "Peter" *(petros)* is a masculine singular word while "rock" *(petra)* is a feminine singular word, so they say that these words obviously aren't referring to the same thing in Jesus' statement. Catholics counter this argument by pointing out that Jesus would have spoken in Aramaic, the common language of Palestine at that time, where "Peter" *(Kepha)* and "rock" *(kepha)* would have been the same.

Some Protestants do believe as Catholics do, however, that Peter is indeed the rock to which Jesus was referring in this passage. Even so, these Protestants say that Peter is only one of the rocks in the church's foundation, along with the other apostles and prophets, as Paul tells us in Ephesians 2:20 that the church is "built upon the foundation of the apostles and prophets, with Christ Jesus himself as the cornerstone." In addition, Peter calls all believers, including himself, "living stones" with Christ as the "cornerstone" (1 Peter 2:5, 6). Protestants also cite that Peter refers to himself as an "elder myself" who exhorts the "elders among you" (1 Peter 5:1), indicating that he is on the same authoritative level as the other church leaders. Furthermore, Paul says that no apostle is inferior to another, including Peter: "I am not at all inferior to these super-apostles, even though I am nothing" (2 Corinthians 12:11).

Moreover, Protestants do not accept the Catholic doctrine of infallibility, believing that Scripture only, not any interpreters of Scripture, is infallible. Even church councils cannot be infallible, Protestants say; rather, decisions should be tested against Scripture before they are followed. And Protestants as a whole don't believe that any man, including the pope, can ever be infallible, except Jesus Christ himself. Even though Peter was inspired several times by the Holy Spirit— instances that Catholics cite in support of his and his successors' infallibility—the other apostles and writers of Scripture were inspired as well. Protestants question what makes Peter's inspiration different from any other spiritual inspiration. In fact, biblical evidence demonstrates that Peter himself wasn't infallible, even concerning matters of faith, such as in Galatians 2:11–14 when Paul rebukes Peter for "not acting consistently with the truth of the gospel" (Galatians 2:14). And, of course, there is the instance foretold by Jesus in which Peter would deny him three times (Luke 22:34), when Peter was obviously not acting in the Spirit. Catholics say that incidents like this, however, demonstrate the human nature of Peter, reflecting the human nature of all people, including popes.

Protestants note that throughout the church's history, some Catholic popes have been involved in scandals, fraud, and other examples of poor morals and integrity. But the Catholic Church insists that the papacy was established by God and is still an office established by God with or without the scandals. Popes may have the gift of infallibility, Catholics say, but, like other humans, do not have a gift of impeccability, or the capacity not to sin.

When you are discussing the topic of Catholic popes and papal infallibility, remember that many Protestant denominations have hierarchies, church councils, and even bishops similar to those in the Catholic Church. Remember also not to discount any messages or information you may hear from either the pope or a Protestant church leader because you may not agree with the established hierarchy of which they are part. As with the other beliefs with which you may disagree, try to understand this topic from both the Catholic and Protestant perspectives.

Relationship Builders

- Catholics believe that Jesus selected Peter as the first pope and that the special authorities given to Peter, including the gift of infallibility, have been passed onto each successive Catholic pope.

  Does either of us believe that Jesus selected Peter as the leader of his church, intending for Peter's successors to oversee the church, a position filled by the Catholic pope?

  How do we feel about Peter's special gifts and authorities, and about the Catholic teaching that they have been passed on to each pope?

*How may our differences of opinion impact our interfaith
relationship?*

- The infallibility authority of the pope is extremely limited, and
only teachings that fall within strict guidelines can be considered
infallible.
*Were we both aware of the restrictions on the pope's infallibility?
How might knowing these limitations affect our perception of this
doctrine?*

- Most Protestants don't accept Peter as the leader of the apostles,
and, likewise, most disagree with Catholics that the popes are Peter's
successors and that they have an authority of infallibility.
*Does either of us believe that Peter was the leader of the apostles,
chosen by Jesus? Why or why not?
What are our personal views regarding the doctrine of infallibility?*

- Many Protestant churches have a hierarchy of authority similar to
that of the Catholic Church.
*What kinds of Protestant church hierarchies have we been aware of?
Do we regard those hierarchies as being any different than the
Catholic Church's structure of the pope and councils of bishops?
Why or why not?*

DIFFERENCE 11

Accepted "Inspired" Books of the Bible

So now, Israel, give heed to the statues and ordinances that I am teaching you to observe, so that you may live to enter and occupy the land that the LORD, the God of your ancestors, is giving you. You must neither add anything to what I command you nor take away anything from it, but keep the commandments of the LORD your God with which I am charging you (Deuteronomy 4:1–2).

When I was about sixteen years old, I had a burning desire to learn more about the Scriptures. Although I heard parts of them in church each week, I wanted to read and try to understand the Scriptures myself. I didn't have a Bible of my own at home, so I went to a local Christian bookstore to buy one. But there I ran into the translation issue. Was the King James Version the "correct" Bible for me to buy as a Catholic? I couldn't remember. So, that's the one I bought, only to find when I arrived home that it indeed was the "wrong" version, so I had to return it. But I never really understood at that time what the controversy was all about. Weren't we all Christians with the same Bible?

You may have run into similar situations about the Protestant Bible versus the Catholic Bible. Which is "right"? Do you understand the differences? What Catholics and Protestants may not realize is that comparable verses between the Catholic and Protestant Bibles are the same. For example, the description of Jesus' birth in Luke 2:1–7 in the Catholic Bible is found in the same place in the Protestant Bible, although the different translations may result in slightly different wordings. All of the Bible quotes in this book are taken from the *New*

Revised Standard Version, Catholic Edition, but the same references can be found in any other translation of the Bible, with the exception of those references made to the so-called questionable books in the Bible. And it is in the inclusion or omission of these books that the Catholic and Protestant Bibles differ and that the debate over what is indeed inspired Scripture rests.

Catholics and Protestants agree on thirty-nine Old Testament books and twenty-seven New Testament books that are indeed divinely inspired. But the Catholic canon and Protestant canon, "canon" referring to the official list of inspired books, differ because of several books and portions of books occurring at the end of the Old Testament, which Catholics refer to as the deuterocanonical (second canon) books, not because they are an additional canon but because they have been questioned, and Protestants refer to as the Apocrypha, meaning writings of questionable authenticity. Found within these books is support for some beliefs that cause conflicts between Catholics and Protestants, such as purgatory and prayers for the dead. In question are seven Old Testament books and two portions of universally accepted Old Testament books:

Tobit
Judith
The Wisdom of Solomon (Wisdom)
Sirach (Ecclesiasticus)
Baruch
1 Maccabees
2 Maccabees
Sections of Esther (10:4 to 16:24)
Sections of Daniel (3:24–90 and chapters 13 and 14)

Therefore, the Catholic canon has forty-six Old Testament books and twenty-seven New Testament books, while the Protestant canon has thirty-nine books in the Old Testament and the same twenty-seven books in the New Testament.

Why do Catholics and Protestants have different canons and therefore different Bibles? The Catholic Old Testament canon is based on a translation of the Hebrew Bible into Greek that is called the Alexandrian translation, or the Septuagint. This translation was completed about 250–125 B.C. and officially accepted by the Council of Trent in 1546. The Protestant Old Testament canon is based on the Palestinian (or Hebrew) translation, which didn't contain the deutero-canonical/apocryphal books. It was established in about A.D. 100 but not widely used until the Protestant Reformation in the sixteenth century. Catholics and Protestants both have arguments as to why their respective canons are correct.

Catholics believe that the Old Testament books in their canon are all inspired because they were all in the original Hebrew Bible translated into the Greek Septuagint, which was the translation of the Bible quoted by Jesus and the New Testament writers. At the Councils of Hippo (A.D. 393) and Carthage (A.D. 397), the Catholic Church—using the authority it believes Christ gave through his apostles and their successors, the Catholic bishops—officially approved all forty-six Old Testament books contained in the Septuagint as being inspired Scripture. At the Council of Trent in 1546, the Catholic Church "formally confirmed the canonicity of all parts of the list fixed in tradition more than a thousand years earlier."[75]

Because the forty-six books in their Old Testament canon were established, used, and accepted by Christians since the early days of the church, Catholics see no reason why the divine authority of any parts of them should be questioned. Catholics believe that Luther reintroduced the Hebrew canon during the Protestant Reformation in support of his defense of salvation by faith alone, rejecting the canon that included the deuterocanonical/apocryphal books because they described practices and beliefs that he didn't support, such as purgatory and praying for the dead. Catholics also point out that Luther added the word "alone" to his German translation of Romans 3:28.

Supposedly, Luther's decision to use the Hebrew translation was also based on his argument that the deuterocanonical/apocryphal Greek books had no Hebrew counterparts; however, the Dead Sea Scrolls

---

[75]R. Lawler, Wuerl, and T. C. Lawler, *Teaching of Christ,* 557.

found at Qumran, an ancient community near the Dead Sea, have revealed Hebrew translations of some of the disputed books. (Nonbiblical items, such as the community rules, were also found with the Scripture, also suggesting that the sacred writings found, including the deuterocanonical/apocryphal books, may not all be inspired Scripture.) Therefore, Catholics see the Old Testament canon used by Protestants as deliberately excluding important pieces of divinely inspired Scripture to support the dogmas and agenda of the Reformation.

Protestants, on the other hand, also believe that their canon comprises the only divinely inspired Scripture. Geisler and MacKenzie say that the true test of canonicity is not historical usage, as Catholics indicate, but instead propheticity, where the books that God intended to be in the Bible all contained prophetic messages.[76] The deuterocanonical/apocryphal books were not written by prophets, and 1 Maccabees 9:27 even says that prophesy had ceased in Israel: "So there was great distress in Israel, such as had not been since the time that prophets ceased to appear among them." And while Jesus and the New Testament writers quoted from the Septuagint, none of them directly quoted from the deuterocanonical or apocryphal books.

Although Protestants do not believe that the deuterocanonical or apocryphal books are inspired, they do acknowledge that these books have historical and devotional value.

As was discussed in *Belief 14: We Believe in the Truth of the Bible and the Importance of Bible Reading* on page 93, Catholics and Protestants accept the inerrancy and infallibility of Scripture and believe that "all scripture is inspired by God and is useful for teaching, for reproof, for correction, and for training in righteousness" (2 Timothy 3:16). Even though just what comprises Scripture has been debated between Catholics and Protestants, you must anchor onto the value you both give to Scripture and concentrate on the majority of the Bible on which you agree, not focus on those parts of Scripture with which you may disagree. In addition, don't think you must exchange one or another

---

[76]Geisler and MacKenzie, *Roman Catholics and Evangelicals,* 166.

of your Bibles for a different translation based on whether it is a Catholic or a Protestant Bible. Each type of Bible has an important value for teaching and learning. Participating in discussions where one of you uses a Catholic Bible and the other uses a Protestant Bible may even add a depth and richness to your conversations that otherwise would not be possible.

Relationship Builders

- Besides slight wording differences due to different translations, Catholic and Protestant Bibles differ in their canons: the Catholic canon contains the deuterocanonical/apocryphal books while the Protestant canon does not.

  Have we traditionally used the Catholic Bible and Protestant Bible respectively?

  Do we have any experiences with the other person's Bible?

  Would we consider learning about the other person's Bible as a growth process for our interfaith relationship?

- Catholics say that Luther and other Protestants embraced a translation of the Bible that supported the agenda of the Protestant Reformation.

  Do we feel that Luther's reasons for promoting the use of the Hebrew translation were sound? Why or why not?

- Protestants hold that the deuterocanonical/apocryphal books are not prophetic books, nor are they quoted in the New Testament.

  What attitudes do we each have toward these disputed books?

  How could these books affect our understanding of certain Catholic doctrines and, in that way, affect our relationship?

- Although Protestants don't accept the deuterocanonical/apocryphal books, they believe they have value nonetheless.

  Even though we may disagree on the source of these books, can we find common ground in the value of their teaching?

DIFFERENCE 12

Catholic Statues and Other "Sacramentals"

Take care and watch yourselves closely, so that you do not act corruptly by making an idol for yourselves, in the form of any figure—the likeness of male or female, the likeness of any animal that is on the earth, the likeness of any winged bird that flies in the air, the likeness of anything that creeps on the ground, the likeness of any fish that is in the water under the earth. And when you look up to the heavens and see the sun, the moon, and the stars, all the host of heaven, do not be led astray and bow down to them and serve them, things that the Lord your God has allotted to all the peoples everywhere under heaven (Deuteronomy 4:15–19).

God did extraordinary miracles through Paul, so that when the handkerchiefs or aprons that had touched his skin were brought to the sick, their diseases left them, and the evil spirits came out of them (Acts 19:11–12).

In his commandment to Moses and the Israelites, God condemned the practice of idolatry, saying: "[Y]ou shall have no other gods before me. You shall not make for yourself an idol, whether in the form of anything that is in heaven above, or that is on the earth beneath, or that is in the water under the earth. You shall not bow down to them or worship them" (Exodus 20:3–5). God makes this command because throughout history, he has witnessed men mistakenly devising and worshipping gods of all sorts, and he wants to establish once and for all that there is only one God.

God's forbiddance of idolatry, or the worship of other gods, is reiterated throughout the Old and New Testaments. Because not practicing idolatry is a biblical command and a biblical truth, Catholics and Protestants alike acknowledge and adhere to this command. Then why, Protestants ask, do Catholics use statues and other symbolic items in their worship? Isn't this an idolatrous practice?

No, Catholics respond, because these items are not the objects of worship. These items are used to represent God, whom we are worshipping, or saints, whom we are honoring for the purpose of drawing closer to God. Referred to as "sacramentals" because they are usually related to one of the Catholic sacraments, these statues and other symbolic items are intended to "keep the presence and thought of God alive and to serve as constant reminders of His love."[77] Schreck elaborates:

> *Sacramentals make use of material objects to remind us of God and to put us into contact with him through our senses. . . . They help us to proclaim the richness of the mystery of Jesus Christ, who desires to use all things he has created to lead us to recognize him and to praise him for his glory revealed in them.*[78]

Early sacramentals were probably objects such as the handkerchiefs and aprons referred to in Acts 19:12. Today, sacramentals include items such as statues, a crucifix, a cross, the rosary, medals, holy water, and holy oil; gestures such as the sign of the cross and genuflection; sacred places, such as shrines; and even sacred times, such as the Exposition of the Blessed Sacrament (when the host, which Catholics believe is the true body of Jesus, is exposed for a period of time in a Catholic church).

---

[77]Altemose, *Why Do Catholics . . . ?*, 102.
[78]Schreck, *Essential Catholic Catechism*, 201–202.

Most Protestants, including my husband, genuinely believe that the use of Catholic sacramentals is a type of idolatry, and are especially bothered by the use of statues and other items dedicated to Mary and the other saints. However, even when a statue or other symbolic item represents God, some Protestants are bothered by their use. Protestants believe that even if a person prays using a statue or other item with the best intentions of not practicing idolatry, man's evil nature makes it too tempting to stray to idolatry. Because man naturally has idolatrous tendencies—seen even today in some people's obsession with money, power, and other "gods"—a person may unconsciously move from venerating God to adoring the relic, and from honoring the relic to worshipping the person it represents.

One notable Protestant theologian compares the Catholic use of these statues and other sacramentals with the Israelites' worship of the golden calf in Exodus 32. However, in this case, the Israelites asked Aaron to "make gods for us, who shall go before us" (Exodus 32:1) because they had rejected the God that had led them out of Egypt and easily reverted to the pagan beliefs of the polytheistic world in which they lived. Unlike these Israelites, however, Catholics do not worship other pagan-like gods, so this comparison is not entirely parallel. (Although some Protestants do feel that Catholics worship Mary and other saints, an issue that is addressed starting on page 128 in *Difference 4: Praying for the Help of Mary and Other Saints*.)

And also unlike the Israelites in Exodus 32, Catholics did not create sacramentals to be gods or idols within themselves. The sacramentals have been created as symbols of God, and sometimes saints, to give Catholics a visual image for their prayers. In a similar way, many Protestants use symbolism and imagery in their prayers. The use of symbolism is more common in some Protestant denominations—such as Episcopalian and Lutheran churches—but forms of symbolism can be found in other Protestant denominations as well. In the Methodist church in which my husband was raised, for example, the congregation had the habit of turning to face the wooden cross on the wall while singing during the offertory. These people were not worshipping the cross itself but Jesus symbolized by the cross. Most Protestants also don't have a problem displaying the nativity scene at Christmas, which contains statues similar to those used by Catholics.

In his essay "Praying with Symbols and Images," author Robert Wise says that it is natural for Christians to use visualization, imagery, and symbolism in their prayers because evidence of these is found throughout both the Old and New Testaments. The ultimate example of this symbolism was offered by God himself in the form of Jesus, the Word made flesh, which is reflected in Christian art and other forms of religious symbolism:

> Christian artists have always known that the meaning of Word became flesh is that God has presented himself in a comprehensible shape. From the beginning, the Christian community found that the ability to visualize the reality of Jesus was a definite asset in worship. . . . Painting a picture for a church wall does not imply a desire to put Jesus or God on a string; rather, we are illustrating the fact that the "Word became flesh." When people visualize Jesus in prayer, they are doing the same thing.[79]

And, Catholics argue, when they use statues and other sacramentals in their prayers, they are likewise using a means to visualize the Word and connect more deeply with God in their prayers. Catholics and Protestants who use symbolism in their prayers are using these visuals as a means of looking "not at what can be seen but at what cannot be seen; for what can be seen is temporary, but what cannot be seen is eternal" (2 Corinthians 4:18).

Recently at our church, we were visited by the "Pilgrim Virgin" statue, a statue of Our Lady of Fatima, named after Mary's appearances in Fatima, Portugal, in 1917. Since 1946, this statue has been traveling around the world. It has been connected with an apparition of Mary over Red Square in Moscow in 1992, and, on more than thirty occasions, it is supposed to have shed human tears. Seeing the people's response to

---

[79]Robert Wise, "Praying With Symbols and Images," in *The Church Divided: The Holy Spirit and a Spirit of Seduction* (South Plainfield, Ill.: Bridge Publishing, Inc., 1986), 74.

the statue that Sunday in church was quite enlightening, for me as well as for Brian.

"People, mostly women, were lined up to look at the statue," says Brian. "That's fine if someone wants to see an article of historical value. But I didn't like seeing the people kneeling and genuflecting in front of the statue. What bothered me even more, though, was the incredible awe I saw in their eyes for the statue only. I saw no awe, no reverence, in their eyes for God."

Seeing how these people reacted around the statue caused me to reflect on how Catholics should approach statues and other sacramentals. As was mentioned in *Difference 4: Praying for the Help of Mary and Other Saints* on page 128, some Catholics are overzealous in their devotion to Mary and other saints, even though the Catholic Church says worship is reserved only for God. Therefore, it is the responsibility of the individual person to make sure that his or her devotion to Mary or another saint does not bleed into worship. The same principle applies here. If someone—Catholic or Protestant—is using a statue or other item in prayer, he or she must take a personal responsibility to not become devoted to the statue or other item, remembering that the item is being used as a symbolic aid to prayer. And Catholics and Protestants alike need to remember that all of their efforts and all of their prayers—even prayers of petitions to saints—need to have the ultimate goal of enriching their worship of the only God, our Lord Jesus Christ.

Relationship Builders

- God's command against idolatry is reiterated in both the Old and New Testaments.
  Do we both agree that idolatry of any kind is a sin?
  Are we both committed to avoiding idolatry in our prayers and daily life?

- Sacramentals are not objects of worship but are symbolic aids to worship.

  For the Catholic: How have I traditionally used sacramentals in my worship?

  Why might my use of sacramentals offend my Protestant partner?

  For the Protestant: What is my attitude toward Catholic sacramentals?

  Can I understand why my partner might use them, or do I consider their use a form of idolatry?

- Symbolism is used in both Catholic and Protestant churches.

  What types of symbolism have we each seen used by Catholics? By Protestants?

  Are there any common symbols used by both denominations?

- All sacramentals and other symbolic items have only one purpose: to bring us closer to God.

  What steps can we take to ensure that the use of sacramentals only enhances our or our partner's worship of God?

Part Three

DISCUSSING
IMPORTANT ISSUES IN OUR
INTERFAITH MARRIAGE

INTRODUCTION

The Hope of One Unified Faith

I will give them one heart, and put a new spirit within them;
I will remove the heart of stone from their flesh and give them
a heart of flesh, so that they may follow my statutes and keep
my ordinances and obey them (Ezekiel 11:19–20).

While the first two sections of *United in Heart, Divided in Faith* were intended to help you understand more deeply the similarities and differences between Catholic and Protestant beliefs, this third section is where you can put what you have learned into practice should your relationship lead into marriage. Through the discussions in this section, you will determine whether or not you are at the same "level" spiritually, talk about the steps you need to take to combine your existing religious traditions while building a faith-based relationship, and discuss issues relating to Christian marriage, church attendance, faith expression, raising children, and family pressures.

Whew! This probably sounds like a lot to handle. But in case no one has told you yet, marriage itself is a huge commitment to handle, involving many decisions, discussions . . . and compromises. Ironically, though, having to work through these interfaith religious issues will likely strengthen your marriage and make you more capable of resolving other conflicts you will encounter. "Religious tolerance is a good foundation for approaching any differences which happen to exist between wife and husband in a marriage," say author John Thomas and reviser David Thomas in their pre-marriage guidebook *Beginning Your Marriage.*[80]

When the two of you become one through the covenant of marriage, you must form a new heart and spirit that are one. You must move forward, united, putting the past behind you: "Do not remember the former things, or consider the things of old" (Isaiah 43:18). This includes putting behind you those religious issues that have divided you. I am not saying you should turn your back on those religious beliefs or practices that have helped to shape the person you've become; I am saying you can't let any of your religious differences cause divisions and cracks in your marriage. If you do, Satan will work at them, attempting to chip away at the strength of your marriage. Because marriage symbolizes Christ's union with the church, Satan delights in weakening and destroying Christian marriages, as will be explained more in *Discussion 1: How Do We Begin to Build a Unified, Faith-Based Relationship?* beginning on page 199.

But whatever you do, don't be intimidated by the gravity of these decisions that you have to make. Take comfort in the fact that each of you has a very useful, God-given tool to help guide you through the process: your conscience. You must follow your conscience, especially regarding topics not explicitly defined or prohibited by Scripture. Your conscience will help you as you are discussing the various facets of these issues and attempting to make decisions that are in line with God's will for your marriage, your lives, and the lives of your children.

Keep in mind that, while these decisions you have to make are difficult, they also present wonderful opportunities for developing your relationship. You have the opportunity to learn how to work together to solve problems. And you have the opportunity to enrich each other through the sharing of your religious traditions while experiencing personal growth in faith and spiritual renewal. Thomas and Thomas tell us that two people with strong religious faith have the best chance of building a successful marriage, even if they are not of the same denomination.[81] I pray that the information that follows is helpful in making your marriage successful. May God guide your discussions and bless your efforts.

---

[80]John L. Thomas, *Beginning Your Marriage,* 8th ed., rev. David M. Thomas (Chicago: ACTA Publications, 1994), 183.

[81]Ibid., 180.

DISCUSSION 1

How Do We Begin to Build a Unified, Faith-Based Relationship?

And the rib that the LORD God had taken from the man he
made into a woman and brought her to the man. Then the man
said, "This at last is bone of my bones and flesh of my flesh;
this one shall be called Woman, for out of Man this one was
taken." Therefore a man leaves his father and his mother
and clings to his wife, and they become one flesh (Genesis
2:22–24).

If you have worked through the first two sections of *United in Heart,
Divided in Faith,* you have come such a long way in building your
interfaith relationship. You have acknowledged similarities and
discussed differences in Catholic and Protestant beliefs. And you have
undoubtedly argued over certain issues as well. All of your efforts have
been God's way of refining you—"See, I have refined you, but not like
silver; I have tested you in the furnace of adversity" (Isaiah 48:10)—and
of preparing you for this even greater challenge: shedding the mind-set
you have each held as individuals in favor of a stronger, unified way of
thinking as a married couple.

Ironically, becoming a unified *couple*—two people who, although still individuals, have become "one flesh" who can think and work together—is one of the hardest challenges for two new spouses. I believe this is especially difficult in today's society when people are marrying at older ages, often after each has lived on his or her own and established a strong, independent character and personality.

Although your individuality may at first be an obstacle to your thinking and acting as a couple, it is the strength and composition of your individual characters and personalities that will ultimately be crucial assets in building a strong, unified, faith-based relationship. Each of your personalities will contribute to making you "one flesh," much as each of a body's parts has a role to play in the one flesh of the body, as Paul explains in 1 Corinthians 12:12: "For just as the body is one and has many members, and all the members of the body, though many, are one body, so it is with Christ." Because your personalities will contribute to the nature of your relationship, you need to take steps now to uncover what exactly comprises each of you individually, the qualities that make each of you you, especially regarding faith and religion.

The best way to start in this discovery process is to determine where each of you stands right now in terms of religious fervor or dedication. Is one of you wholly committed to Christ in all that you do, while the other is a "weekend Christian"? Or are both of you equally focused on God? *Discussion 2: Are We Unequally Yoked?* on page 205 provides a series of questions and other insights to help you evaluate where you each stand in your walk with God.

In order to build your relationship, you will each also need to have an insider's perspective of the other person's religion, a vantage that you can only get by submersing yourself in his or her religious tradition, through a process referred to by Thomas and Thomas as "mutual unlocking."[82] Here are some suggestions for actively learning about each other's religious tradition and ultimately strengthening your marriage:

---

[82]Ibid., 177.

- Support and respect each other's religion and individual faith practices.
- Attend a church or church-related activities in each other's denomination.
- Explore activities that you can pursue as a couple or individually at one or the other of your churches.
- Talk to your partner's family or friends about your partner's religion, if these people are willing to discuss religion without judgment and without heat.
- Meet with a pastor and/or priest to discuss your religious issues and concerns receive answers to any questions you may have.
- Pray together or read the Bible together and discuss what you read.
- Consider what faith practices and traditions you may be able to incorporate into your home and nuclear family.
- Read books and other literature concerning the doctrines of your partner's religion.

As you are going through this process of mutual discovery, start to think of ways you can combine your personal religious traditions into your faith practice as a couple. Praying is one good example. In our house, we traditionally pray before meals not only to thank God for the food but to thank him for other blessings as well, along with offering certain petitions of need to him. You also may want to create special celebrations for just the two of you, such as the anniversary of your engagement, your first date, and, of course, your wedding. Invite God into these celebrations through prayer and open hearts: "In all your ways acknowledge him, and he will make straight your paths" (Proverbs 3:6). (For more suggestions on forming new faith traditions, see *Discussion 5: How Will We Express Our Faith as a Married Couple?* on page 224.)

A word of warning, though. As you begin to cultivate your interfaith relationship, strengthen your marriage, and grow in your faith of God, you are likely to also see an increase of Satan's influence in your life. Because the marriage covenant reflects Christ's unity with the church, Satan desires to break down the marriage testimonies to that unity. Satan's influence in a marriage is most often subtle and can take forms such as:

- Picking on each other over really insignificant things.
- Focusing on negative qualities in each other, including physical characteristics or personality traits.
- Bickering over misunderstandings between you.
- Having a "wandering eye" toward members of the opposite sex who you think might make you happier or understand or appreciate you more than your spouse.

Because you know your relationship most intimately, you can best identify the weaknesses that Satan may try to exploit. And you can learn the times when he's most likely to strike. Larry and Kathy Miller, who minister to married couples together, have noticed that they tend to argue with each other the day that they have an event scheduled.[83] I've noticed that Brian and I tend to fight more when I've had a successful day working on this book, and also on Sundays after we've had a spiritually renewing experience together at church. Trying to anticipate the times that Satan may try to wheedle his way in between you and the tactics he may use to drive you apart can help you to resist his influence. If you do feel he is influencing you, "resist the devil, and he will flee from you" (James 4:7). Just say something out loud like "Get out of here, Satan! You won't be successful in disrupting this situation. I won't turn against God." But beware that this will only dismiss Satan temporarily, like swatting at a bee or a fly. Know that he will come buzzing back at a more opportune moment, so stay alert. (See also *Belief 8: We Believe in the Existence of Satan and Hell* on page 59 for more about Satan and his evil influence.)

Beginning to build your faith-based relationship as a couple, then, involves first finding out what each of you is bringing to the table for

---

[83]Larry Miller and Kathy Miller, *What's in the Bible for . . .*[TM] *Couples* (Lancaster, Pa.: Starburst Publishers, 2000), 278.

the relationship. Although the Catholic Church doesn't advocate interfaith or mixed marriages, it still believes they can succeed when the couple places "in common what they have received from their respective [religious] communities, and learn[s] from each other the way in which each lives in fidelity to Christ."[84] Above all, keep Christ at the center of all of your efforts, as is said so well by Graham: "Put Christ first in your life and then first in your marriage and you will have a bond between yourself, your mate, and the Lord that no one can break."[85]

Relationship Builders

- If you both have strong, independent personalities, becoming a truly united couple may be particularly difficult for you.
  Which of our personal characteristics may be obstacles to our becoming a united couple?
  How can we turn these obstacles into assets that can strengthen our interfaith relationship?

- "Mutual unlocking" is the process through which you can learn about each other's religious tradition by actually experiencing elements of it.
  What efforts can we make or what kinds of activities can we participate in together that will help us to better understand each other's religion and religious practices?

- Each couple needs to find personal ways to practice their faith.
  What are some special days or events that we can celebrate together with God?

- Satan is a constant threat to the unity of married Christian couples.
  What are the weaknesses in our personalities or relationship that Satan may try to use against us?
  When are the times that he is most likely to strike?

---

[84]*CCC,* 408.
[85]Graham, *Unto the Hills,* 119.

DISCUSSION 2

Are We Unequally Yoked?

Do not be mismatched with unbelievers. For what part-nership is there between righteousness and lawlessness? Or what fellowship is there between light and darkness? What agreement does Christ have with Beliar? Or what does a believer share with an unbeliever? What agree-ment has the temple of God with idols? (2 Corinthians 6:14–16).

My husband and I first began our relationship as a long-distance relationship when he was living in Florida and I was living in Pennsylvania. What we knew about each other consisted primarily of what we had shared over the telephone and through letters. The same applied to religion. Neither of us had yet had the opportunity to see the other's "faith in action." What we knew collectively was that I was Catholic, Brian was Protestant, and we both attended church regularly. Consequently, some of Brian's family and friends were concerned about the long-term viability of the relationship, fearing that he and I weren't at the same level spiritually. Some of them went so far as to advise him against pursuing the relationship, saying that I wasn't a Christian because I was Catholic.

Luckily for me, Brian didn't listen to their advice, instead waiting to meet me in person and getting to know me better, thereby understanding that I am indeed a Christian. Through our discussions, we realized another important aspect: In spite of our differences in religious practices and beliefs, we are both Christians who are at relatively the same level spiritually. We both believe in the importance of Christ's role in our daily lives and invite him into our lives through daily prayers. We are not uncomfortable praying together. We both equally believe in the importance of attending church regularly. We both feel it is of the utmost importance to teach our son about Christ. We believe in the importance of Bible reading. We give the same level of importance to all things Christian, which is why I can say we are at the same level spiritually, even though we hold slightly different views of certain aspects of religious traditions and practices.

You and your partner must also determine whether you are at the same level spiritually so that you can most effectively address other interfaith issues in your relationship. To help you establish where you each are in your walk with God, try asking yourselves the following questions. It may help if you write your answers on separate pieces of paper and then compare your answers when you are through.

1. Do I consider myself a Christian? Do I believe that Jesus Christ is my Savior?

2. Do I attend church each week?

3. If no, why not?

4. If yes, do I attend because I believe this will enhance my spiritual life or because I feel obligated?

5. When in church, do I pay attention to the service or Mass, or do I daydream?

6. Do I try to pray regularly?

7. Do I read the Bible regularly?

8. Do I see Christ in little things throughout the day, or do I only think about him in the morning and evening, or perhaps only on Sundays, or perhaps not at all?

9. Do I genuinely want to grow in my relationship with Christ? Do I do anything specific to enhance this growth?

10. Do I honestly want to educate my children about Christ, or don't I really care about that?

There's no scoring key or other easy way for you to determine whether you are at the same spiritual level. You both need just to compare your honest answers and discuss with each other your personal relationship with God.

If you both feel you are at the same spiritual level after discussion, congratulations! You can support each other as you both move forward in your relationship with God. You can also anchor your relationship in this strength while you go on to address the other issues in your inter-faith relationship.

If one of you feels that you aren't as spiritually dedicated or "advanced" as the other, however, this doesn't mean that your relationship is doomed. It just means that you need to spend a little extra time understanding and cultivating this aspect of your relationship.

If one of you is not a Christian, then perhaps you need to consider what kind of a future this relationship will hold. The purpose of this life is to continually grow in our relationship with God through the support of other Christians, including one's spouse. Having a spouse that isn't a Christian likely will hamper your spiritual growth. In Deuteronomy 7:3–4, God warns the Israelites not to intermarry with pagan foreigners "for that would turn away your children from following me, to serve other gods" (Deuteronomy 7:4). Even wise Solomon erred in this respect by loving his pagan wives so much that they "turned away his heart after other gods; and his heart was not true to the Lord his God, as was the heart of his father David" (1 Kings 11:4). Don't remain in a relationship that is going to hamper your relationship with God or cause you to sin against God.

However, if you are both Christians, one being more deeply involved in religion than the other, you need to determine whether this difference in your spiritual levels will hamper your relationship.

Remember that when you marry, you are both joining together in a covenant with God. Therefore, you need him to take an active role in your marriage in order for it to be able to weather the rough times and continue to grow. You need to be sure that the disparity in your spiritual levels will not hinder your marital growth or your personal relationship with God.

Here are some suggestions for discussing how your differences in religious fervor may impact your marriage:

- Discuss your religious backgrounds and why one of you may have lost—or never had—interest in religion, while the other is more religiously committed.

- Talk about the importance of religion in your lives, or why it might not be so important.

- Exchange opinions about how your difference in religious commitment could impact your interfaith relationship and any children you might have.

- Bring into the open any preconceived notions either of you has that the other will change beliefs and/or religious fervor at some point. Is it realistic to expect such changes? How could these changes impact your spiritual health?

- Don't try to force your beliefs on each other. Don't ridicule each other for beliefs or lack of beliefs.

- Make honest efforts to learn about each other's religion and why you may or may not be committed to it.

Through honest and open communication, and God's guidance, you will be able to discern based on your discussions whether or not your interfaith relationship is worth pursuing.

Relationship Builders

- Answering some basic questions about your attitude toward Christianity can help you determine your levels of religious commitment.

Discussion 2

*Did answering these questions give us each a clearer understanding
of where we stand today in our relationship with God?*
*Through this exercise, did we learn anything new or surprising
about our religious commitments?*
Do we consider ourselves to be on the same level spiritually?

- This exercise may have affirmed that you are both Christians, or it
may have revealed that one of you is not a Christian.
  *Were we able to determine that we are both Christians? If not, do I,
  the unbeliever, have an interest in becoming a Christian?*
  *How will one of us not being a Christian impact our interfaith
  relationship and the Christian's walk with God?*

- One of you may be more "advanced" in terms of spiritual growth
than the other.
  *Do we think it will be a problem for us to be at different levels
  spiritually?*
  *Are we committed to both moving forward in our relationship with
  God, albeit from different starting points?*

- Your different spiritual levels can have a huge impact on your
relationship.
  *Are we honestly committed to trying to uncover why one of us might
  be more religiously committed than the other?*
  *Can we be honest about how this disparity may impact our marriage
  and our children?*
  *Do we have the courage to walk away from this relationship if we
  believe that God is leading us in different directions?*

DISCUSSION 3

What About Our Marriage?

Two are better than one, because they have a good reward for their toil. For if they fall, one will lift up the other; but woe to one who is alone and falls and does not have another to help. Again, if two lie together, they keep warm; but how can one keep warm alone? And though one might prevail against another, two will withstand one. A threefold cord is not quickly broken (Ecclesiastes 4:9–12).

Marriage is a noble vocation, one to which most Christians are called and one which was established and blessed by God in the first marriage between Adam and Eve. (See Genesis 2:18 and 1:28.) In this first marriage, and in all marriages after, God has promised to unite himself with married couples in "a threefold cord," supporting and sustaining them through both good and bad times. In addition, Jesus also showed his blessing of marriage by choosing the wedding at Cana of Galilee as the site of his first miracle (John 2:1–11). In Mark 10:9, Jesus also emphasizes the importance of marriage in God's eyes by describing the indissolubility of the marriage bond: " 'Therefore what God has joined together, let no one separate.'" (See also Mark 10:2–8 and Matthew 19:3–6.) By explaining through Paul in Ephesians

5:22–33 that marriage is a visible sign of Christ's union with his church, God has elevated marriage to a sacramental level, the Catholic Church believes. (See also "Sacrament of Matrimony" in *Difference 7: Catholic Sacraments Described* on page 157.)

If you have established your common beliefs and discussed your differences and have decided to commit to each other in marriage, that's wonderful! With this decision, however, comes even more issues that you must address regarding your interfaith wedding. Your life together had been a melding of two different faith backgrounds, and there is no reason why your marriage ceremony can't reflect your differences along with your united, Christian relationship. And this can be done within the requirements established by the Catholic Church for what it refers to as "mixed marriages." (Because requirements for marriage in a Protestant church can vary among Protestant denominations, this chapter will focus primarily on marriages between a Catholic and a Protestant being held in a Catholic church. If you are interested in being married in a Protestant church, contact the appropriate pastor or minister for the particular denominational requirements.)

Before a couple can receive the sacrament of matrimony in a Catholic church, they must know and accept the Catholic Church's biblically based marriage requirements:

1. *The man and woman must freely consent to enter into marriage, must be legally able to make this commitment, and must be baptized as Christians.* Jesus says in Mark 16:16, " 'The one who believes and is baptized will be saved.' " As was mentioned in *Belief 10: We Believe in the Importance of Baptism* beginning on page 71, Catholics and Protestants both believe a person needs to be baptized. Catholics believe that a person can only be baptized once; therefore, the Catholic Church does recognize non-Catholic Christian baptisms as being valid. If, for some reason, one or both of you was never baptized, you must receive this sacrament before receiving the sacrament of matrimony. Contact your priest or minister for information

about becoming baptized through the Catholic Rite of Christian Initiation of Adults (RCIA) program or a similar program at a Protestant church.

2. *The man and woman must promise to be faithful for life.* Paul tells us, "[A] married woman is bound by the law to her husband as long as he lives. . . . she will be called an adulteress if she lives with another man while her husband is alive" (Romans 7:1, 3).

3. *The marriage cannot be dissolved and will only end upon the death of one of the spouses.* Jesus says, " '[W]hat God has joined together, let no one separate. . . . Whoever divorces his wife, except for unchastity, and marries another commits adultery' " (Matthew 19: 6, 9). Because it reflects Christ's union with his Church, marriage is an indissoluble covenant.

4. *The couple must be open to having children.* In Genesis 1:28, God commands Adam and Eve to "be fruitful and multiply." A couple must be willing to accept children as a gift from God.

Several months before a scheduled marriage, the Catholic Church requires engaged couples to attend pre-marriage classes, called Pre-Cana classes, after the location of Jesus' first public miracle. These classes, which may be concentrated on a weekend or held once a week for several weeks, cover topics such as communication, spirituality, sexuality, parenting, finances, unity, and even interfaith marriage. Most Protestant churches also offer similar programs or pre-marriage counseling for engaged couples. Much as the goal of this book, the pre-marriage classes and pre-marriage counseling are intended to help couples work out their differences before they are married to avoid conflicts within the marriage relationship and the weakening, or even severing by divorce, of the marriage bond.

In order for a couple to continue practicing the Catholic faith as a family, their marriage needs to be recognized as valid. Normally, this means being married in a Catholic church by a Catholic priest, with assistance by a Protestant minister, if the couple chooses. This could be in the home church of the Catholic party, another Catholic church that the couple has attended together, or even a "neutral" Catholic church to which neither has affiliation. In some circumstances, the couple can receive permission from the bishop to be married in a non-Catholic church by a non-Catholic minister. In this case, a priest might assist in the ceremony. Marriages in a non-church location, such as in a garden or a restaurant, are not normally permitted but may be allowed in a situation such as if an elderly grandmother can only attend the wedding if it is held in her backyard. A Catholic priest should officiate at even those weddings held outside a church. Also, couples are not permitted by the Catholic Church to be married by a judge or a justice of the peace. In addition, the Catholic Church does not allow a couple to be married twice, in two separate services, nor does it allow the Catholic marriage ritual and a non-Catholic marriage ritual to be celebrated together.

Depending on the diocese, a Catholic may have to receive permission from the bishop before marrying a non-Catholic, based upon requirements in the 1983 Code of Canon Law. This church law also requires:

1. The Catholic to "remove dangers of defecting from the faith" and to try to "do all in his or her power in order that all the children be baptized and brought up in the Catholic Church." (See also *Discussion 6: In What Religion Will We Raise Our Children?* on page 229.)

2. The Protestant to be aware of the commitments of the Catholic.

3. Both people to know and accept "the purposes and essential properties of marriage."[86]

Be sure to check with your priest to see how these laws affect mixed marriages in your diocese.

---

[86]*The Code of Canon Law* (1983), Book IV, Part I: The Sacraments, Title VII: Marriage, Chapter VI: Mixed Marriages, www.ourladywarriors.org/canon/c0840–1165.htm#par2307. Accessed 15 Sept. 2002.

Assuming your wedding takes place in a Catholic church, you have several options from which to choose to make your ceremony unique. You can select to have a simple Catholic wedding ceremony, with Scripture readings, prayers, songs, and the marriage ceremony itself. Or you can choose to have these elements integrated into a full Catholic Mass, including the sacrament of Holy Eucharist. However, as was mentioned on page 147 in the "Sacrament of Holy Communion" section of *Difference 7: The Catholic Sacraments Described,* the Catholic Church doesn't allow intercommunion with non-Catholics because of the differences in beliefs regarding the substance of the Eucharist. Therefore, the non-Catholic partner, as well as the non-Catholic family members and guests, would not be permitted to participate in the sacrament of Holy Eucharist. One writer compares this restriction to the wedding ceremony itself: "Christian churches won't marry a couple unless the couple shares the church's beliefs about marriage and promises to abide by them. Roman Catholic Christian churches offer the Eucharist to people who share the church's belief about the Eucharist and promises to receive it in the proper spirit."[87]

When Brian and I wed, we chose to be married in a Catholic church that we had been attending for several months together, near to where we both lived. We wanted to have the marriage officiated by a priest from that church whom we both liked and who was supportive of our Catholic-Protestant relationship. For our wedding itself, we chose to only have the Catholic wedding ceremony. Brian was willing to have a full Catholic Mass, but I opted for the ceremony only to avoid making him and the non-Catholic members of our families feel uncomfortable. We also integrated some Protestant Christian elements into the ceremony by having the pianist play songs by contemporary Christian artists such as Michael W. Smith, along with classical and traditional wedding selections. In addition, we had both Catholic and non-Catholic members of our families participate in the wedding as attendants and readers.

Involving various members of your family in your wedding ceremony as well may be a good way for you to celebrate the unity of

---

[87] www3.cems.umn.edu/~glaser/psst.htm.

you and your families. You could also choose to light a unity candle, where your mothers each light a smaller candle that you will use to light a larger candle, also symbolizing the joining of you and your families in unity. Another Catholic wedding tradition is for the bride to offer flowers to Mary while an appropriate song such as *Ave Maria* is played, the bride seeking Mary's help in her new role as wife and, potentially, mother.

Whatever options you choose, you should reassure the non-Catholic guests and family members who will be attending your wedding that they shouldn't feel obligated or pressured into participating in the Mass or ceremony more than they feel comfortable. They shouldn't feel obligated to say prayers with which they don't agree, or to kneel when they would rather sit. Nor should they feel they should participate in the sacrament of Holy Eucharist, should the ceremony include a Mass, for reasons presented earlier. You might want to include an informational sheet with your wedding invitations, or even create a web site, that explains the various elements you will be incorporating into your wedding and the meanings behind them. Through being open about the options you choose and the decisions you make, you invite your families into the Christian unity that you have established between yourselves.

When planning your wedding, don't forget to check with your church at least six months before you want to be married to see what specific requirements the diocese may have for interfaith marriages, to schedule Pre-Cana classes, to reserve the church, and to seek answers to any other questions you may have. Above all, remember that what you are entering in marriage is a sacred covenant with each other and with God. Keep this as your focus, directing all of your efforts toward this celebration of unity, and you will have a beautiful and blessed wedding.

Relationship Builders

- The Catholic Church has requirements, with which most Protestants would agree, that you must accept before being married in a Catholic church.

Are we each legally free to marry as baptized Christians?
Do we intend to remain faithful?
Is divorce an option for us when circumstances become difficult?
Do we both want to have children?

- You need to choose a church in which to be married and a priest and/or pastor to officiate at your wedding.
  What options are available to us?
  How do we feel about each of the available options?

- A Catholic wedding can include a full Mass with the sacrament of Holy Eucharist or a ceremony only. Also, you can creatively personalize and incorporate several different elements into a Catholic wedding, including:

  Music

  Attendants

  Readers

  Unity candle

  Flowers for Mary

  Would we both prefer a Mass or a ceremony only?
  Which elements would we like to have in our wedding?
  In what ways can we personalize these elements to make them uniquely reflect our Christian unity?

- You should strive to make both families feel comfortable with the wedding celebration.
  What steps can we take to bring our families together in heart and spirit, as well as body, for this celebration of our unity?

DISCUSSION 4

What Church Should We Attend After We Marry?

Now I appeal to you, brothers and sisters, by the name of our Lord Jesus Christ, that all of you be in agreement and that there be no divisions among you, but that you be united in the same mind and the same purpose. For it has been reported to me by Chloe's people that there are quarrels among you, my brothers and sisters. What I mean is that each of you says, "I belong to Paul," or "I belong to Apollos," or "I belong to Cephas," or "I belong to Christ." Has Christ been divided? Was Paul crucified for you? Or were you baptized in the name of Paul? (1 Corinthians 1:10–13).

"When asked what religion I am, I avoid being associated with a denomination and simply respond that I am a 'Christian,' " says Brian. "I feel strongly that religion is an expression practiced and shared by men, while faith is a personal belief in God."

While Brian's perspective is true, as a married interfaith couple you will still need to decide in which Christian community you want to practice your faith or, more pointedly, what church you will attend. Will you attend a Catholic or a Protestant church together? Will you each attend a church of your own denomination separately? Should you convert to the other person's religion? Or will you stop going to church altogether?

With so many choices, how do you possibly decide? In our family, Brian strongly believes that a family unit needs to attend one church together. Because I want to be in an environment where I can receive the Catholic sacraments, and attending Mass is a precept of the Catholic Church (see the *Catechism,* 2041ff), and because Brian doesn't disagree with Catholics on any major theological issues, we have chosen primarily to attend a Catholic church together. We do also periodically attend Protestant worship services. However, Brian's Protestant background and belief systems are important to him, so even though he attends a Catholic church, he has no intention of converting to Catholicism.

Because Brian and I have established that we have the same core Christian faith beliefs that are reflected in the Catholic Church, attending a Catholic church together works for us. But this may not be the right option for you. Only the two of you can pick the solution that will work best for your interfaith relationship. To help you make this important decision, I've listed below some of the options available to you, along with positive and negative aspects of each:

Option 1: *Attend a church in one of your denominations.* This option, which is the one we've selected, is where you would both attend either a Catholic or a Protestant church together.

Positive: One of you will feel comfortable maintaining the religious practices with which you feel most comfortable. You will also be able to teach the other about your religion while you are both actively participating in it and building a unified faith within the family.

Negative: Just as one of you will feel comfortable with this option, the other may feel uncomfortable. One of you will be leaving a familiar church environment and may have difficulty worshipping in the new style. You also may not feel entirely a part of the new church, especially if you cannot participate fully in the church service. My husband often feels left out because, as a non-Catholic, he is not permitted to participate in the sacrament of Holy Communion. If this is the option you choose, however, you can balance your attendance at one church denomination with faith practices from the other denomination. (For suggestions, see *Discussion 5: How Will We Express Our Faith as a Married Couple?* on page 224.)

Option 2: *Find a "neutral" church.* This option is essentially to go to a church within a new denomination that incorporates familiar elements of each person's religion. One example would be to attend an Episcopalian church, which is a Protestant denomination that incorporates rituals similar to those found in a Catholic church. Another is to attend a denominationally neutral Christian church, a Protestant church centered on biblical teaching without denominational rituals.

Positive: This church would be a compromise, each of you meeting halfway in an environment that doesn't favor one or the other of your religious denominations.

Negative: Because you are both leaving familiar church denominations, either or both of you may feel that you are betraying your respective faith tradition, or you may simply miss your old style of worship. You may also feel uncomfortable in the new environment, making it difficult for you to worship. And if your church is denominational, you may have trouble accepting the doctrines of the new denomination. In addition, your families may resent your decision. (See *Discussion 7: How Do We Respond to Questions, Comments, and Pressures from Our Families and Friends?* on page 236 for more about handling family concerns.)

Option 3: *Attend two churches together permanently.* You could decide to permanently attend two different churches together, either attending two services each week, or alternating weeks between the churches.

Positive: This option enables each of you to keep your familiar religious practices while actively learning about the other's religion. Your efforts will not minimize your religious differences but instead honor the uniqueness of each religion.

Negative: If you choose to attend two services each week, this option will essentially double the time you are used to spending in community worship. Consequently, one or both of you may feel overextended and may not want to maintain this practice long term, potentially leading to conflict, resentment, and the desire to return to your original churches. If time commitments are concerns for you but you are still interested in this option, you may want to consider attending two churches, alternating weeks between the churches.

Option 4: *Attend two churches together temporarily.* You could attend different churches together, with the intention of selecting one with which you both feel comfortable and which you could then attend together permanently.

Positive: Short term, neither of you is giving up your familiar religious practices, and you each have the opportunity to actively learn about the other person's religion.

Negative: Again, you will essentially be doubling the time you normally spend in church, which may make you feel overextended and lead to feelings of resentment and other problems. And you will eventually have to choose one religious denomination over the other, which may cause conflicts if you both remain strongly committed to your respective religious denomination and practices. Through this option, you may also be postponing a decision that you should really make up-front.

Option 5: *Attend two churches separately.* You could each remain involved in your own denomination, attending separate churches.

Positive: Neither of you has to give up the religious practices with which you are most familiar and comfortable.

Negative: This option reduces the amount of time a couple spends together, especially in the crucial area of community worship. And with this option, you wouldn't be building a unified faith, at least in terms of community worship; this lack of unity could potentially weaken your relationship, making you less able to handle future conflicts. Selecting this option may also create problems when deciding how to religiously educate your children. (See also *Discussion 6: In What Religion Will We Raise Our Children?* on page 229.)

Option 6: *Convert to the other person's religion.* One of you could officially change to the other person's religion. However, this option would only work if the converting spouse genuinely believes that the conversion will enhance his or her relationship with God.

Positive: Both of you would now be of the same Christian denomination, potentially alleviating many of the problems and issues faced by Christian interfaith couples.

Negative: Because one person is giving up a religious tradition, that person may have feelings of resentment and a sense that he or she is abandoning an essential element of who he or she is. These negative feelings could then bleed into other aspects of the relationship, having an overall negative impact on the relationship.

Option 7: *Stop attending church altogether.* Because of the difficulty in making this decision, some couples may be tempted to stop going to church to avoid having to make a decision.

Positive: None.

Negative: Initially, a positive aspect of this option could be thought to be the avoidance of religious conflicts. However, not addressing these conflicts doesn't resolve them; rather it buries them, letting them simmer and gather energy beneath the surface, just waiting to erupt into an enormous problem for your relationship. Further, choosing this option goes against the advice of Hebrews 10:24–25: "[L]et us consider how to provoke one another to love and good deeds, not neglecting to meet together, as is the habit of some."

UNITED IN HEART, DIVIDED IN FAITH

Another negative aspect of this option is that both of you would be turning your back on religious traditions that have helped to shape the character with which you each fell in love. In addition, eliminating church attendance would leave a void in your life that could potentially be filled with a harmful addiction, practice, or other evil influence. You would also be missing valuable opportunities for interacting with other Christians, participating in church activities and rituals, religiously educating your children, and worshipping God as a community. Not attending church may also cause you to become slack in your personal prayers, jeopardizing your relationship with God and exposing you to harm from evil influences. This option is not recommended.

Here are some questions and factors to take into consideration when trying to decide what church to attend:

- *Does this church teach from the Bible?*
- *Does this church offer the kinds of programs that will strengthen your marriage and family?*
- *Don't wait to find the "perfect" church—otherwise you may never join a church!*
- *Look for a church that desires to spread the gospel to those who don't know God.*

Deciding what church to attend will not be easy. And as you can see by the many references to other chapters, this decision will affect many other aspects of your interfaith marriage. When you are making this important decision, you need to keep in mind the words of the apostle Paul in 1 Corinthians 1:10–13. You need to remember that in looking for a church, you are searching for a style of worship with which you are both comfortable; you are not compromising your core Christian faith beliefs. By choosing one church over another, by following "Paul" instead of "Apollos," you are not turning your back on God but are simply seeking the best community environment in which you can both most effectively worship him.

Relationship Builders

- The religious elements, practices, and traditions that a certain church denomination offers may be an important factor in deciding what church to attend.
  In what denomination would we each feel comfortable worshipping?
  Would we consider attending a "neutral" church?

- Other available options are to attend two churches together, either permanently or temporarily, or attend two churches separately.
  Does either of us feel strongly about attending church together or
  separately?

- Conversion is also an option to consider, although it must be done for the purpose of enhancing one's relationship with God, not as a potentially dangerous compromise.
  Is either of us considering converting to the other's religion?
  What are our motivations for wanting to convert?

- Not attending church is, unfortunately, an option some couples choose to avoid making a decision.
  Are either or both of us frustrated enough to consider not attending
  church at all?
  Are we willing to pray together to overcome this frustration?

DISCUSSION 5

How Will We Express Our Faith as a Married Couple?

[Jesus said,] "Every kingdom divided against itself is laid waste, and no city or house divided against itself will stand" (Matthew 12:25).

When we were engaged, Brian and I had a bad experience one Christmas Eve. We started our celebration with the traditional Christmas Eve meal at my grandmother's house at five o'clock. Then we raced to his parent's church for the Christmas Eve service at seven o'clock, after which we were supposed to open presents at his parent's house. The service ran long, which threw me into a panic because I was due at my parent's house by eleven o'clock to head to Midnight Mass at my parent's church. The pressures of the evening were immense, and I ended up leaving his parent's house in tears right after they arrived home from church. Everyone was upset that evening, and some residual hurt feelings still persist to this day.

That night, we had unsuccessfully tried to hold on to all of those faith traditions of our families that we had practiced when we were single, not to mention avoid hurting anyone's feelings by not keeping with our old traditions. This fiasco was our rude awakening to the fact that, as a married couple, we had to establish and practice traditions of our own and make decisions that were right for us as a couple, not to run ourselves ragged trying to please everyone else. Putting each other and your needs as a couple first reflects your commitment in love to each other and your love for God. The Bible says, "You shall love the LORD your God with all your heart, and with all your soul, and with all your might" (Deuteronomy 6:5). By loving each other in this way and elevating each other's needs above the wants and needs of others, you also show your love for God, who is joined with you in your marriage covenant.

As a couple, you need to consider ways through which you can express your faith as a couple and grow in Christian unity. The challenge is to identify and participate in activities and develop family traditions that can help each of you grow in faith, while staying committed to keeping each other happy and reflecting your love for God.

Many of the primary faith decisions that you will need to make as a couple concern your religious practice as a family. You need to decide what church to attend together (see *Discussion 4: What Church Should We Attend After We Marry?* on page 217) and how to religiously educate your children (see *Discussion 6: In What Religion Will We Raise Our Children* on page 229). Aside from these decisions, you also have other options available to you to strengthen and spiritually enrich your inter-faith relationship.

You need to think about how to express your faith in your home. Growing up, each of your families likely practiced their faith in different ways. Perhaps each person in your family expressed his or her faith privately. You may have prayed together for meals but prayed individually at other times. Maybe your family didn't have any regular faith practices, aside from attending church together. Or perhaps you didn't even attend church as a family. On the other hand, your family may have been very outwardly religious, praying together often and reading the Bible aloud regularly. Whatever the case, discuss the faith traditions of the homes in which you were raised, and then talk about which of those elements, if any, you'd like to incorporate into your household. There may even be new faith traditions that you'd like to add to your family. Do you feel you would benefit from praying together often throughout the day? Perhaps you'd like to start a devotional/prayer program together. Maybe you'd like to do simple, daily readings from Scripture, either to yourselves or to each other, and then discuss how the Scripture could apply to your lives. Look for personal ways in which to bring your unified Christian faith alive within your home.

Seek ways to express your faith outside your home. Probably the most abundant opportunities will be offered by your church. Would you enjoy attending a Bible study together? Perhaps your church has outreach ministries in which you would both enjoy participating. You may even want to look into missionary trips that you can take together. As a couple, you can help spread the gospel through evangelization while, at the same time, building and stabilizing your own relationship by working together.

In your efforts to identify and pursue faith-based activities that you can do together, however, don't be misled into thinking you can't continue to participate in activities individually. Sometimes, couples make the mistake of throwing their entire selves into a relationship, losing themselves and their individualities within the relationship. Consequently, they become unable to define themselves as people outside of the relationship and lose the personal qualities that attracted themselves to each other in the first place. Through abandoning their individual selves, sometimes unknowingly, couples also lose the benefits that their individual strengths can bring to the relationship. So don't be afraid to pursue separate activities and participate in different groups. Just be careful not to become so involved in separate activities that you rarely see each other. Over a period of time, the prolonged absences and resulting lack of intimate time together could have a detrimental effect on the relationship. Keep your lines of communication open and seek a balance of activities with which you are both comfortable.

You will also need to consider how you want to present yourself to your families as a unified couple. As will be discussed further in

Discussion 7: How Do We Respond to Questions, Comments, and Pressures From Our Families? beginning on page 236, your families may not be entirely pleased with or supportive of your interfaith relationship. To help quell criticisms from them, you need to present a unified front, letting them know that, in spite of some different beliefs you may hold, you are united in your faith. If you show others that there are disagreements or chasms between you, some families may try to exploit those weaknesses, encouraging one of you to attend the church you've always attended or even putting down your partner's religion or faith practices. This type of pressure could be damaging as you struggle to establish and build a unified Christian relationship.

And don't forget to address the celebration of holidays, especially religious holidays, which will present a special challenge for you as an interfaith couple. You may want to continue practicing established holiday traditions with your families, but be sure to discuss them with each other and evaluate them to see if that is what is best for your relationship. Some families may try to coerce you into going to this church, or visiting this person, and so on, but, as with other issues in your relationship, you may need to take a stand of solidarity, perhaps even opposing your families' wishes. You need to make decisions that are right for you. Don't let obligations and other pressures force you into participating in activities that may ultimately damage the relationship you are working so hard to establish. Remember, once you are married, you are committed to each other. Your new, nuclear family is what should come first. And as you are building your new family, keep your eyes open for new traditions you can practice and unique ways in which you can celebrate special times together.

Ultimately, everything you do, every activity in which you participate, should glorify God through praise, worship, and thanksgiving.

Relationship Builders

- We hear repeated over and over throughout the Bible the importance of loving God.

  In what ways can placing the needs of each other before the needs or desires of others reflect our love for God?

  Can we understand that some of our relationship difficulties may be a result of not surrendering our love to each other and to God?

- Couples need to identify and pursue activities that express their unified Christian faith both inside and outside the home, both as a couple and as individuals.

  What faith practices or traditions would we like to incorporate into our home life?

  What kinds of programs does our church offer in which we could participate?

  When we think of certain activities, do we picture ourselves participating in them as a couple or as individuals?

- Managing the celebration of holidays is a difficult challenge for most couples, especially those who are trying to merge the faith practices of two religions.

  How has each of our families traditionally celebrated holidays?

  Which of these traditions, if any, would we like to maintain?

  What are some new holiday traditions we could establish for our nuclear family?

- Christians need to ensure that all of their activities and efforts serve to praise, worship, and thank God.

  Has either of us forgotten about glorifying God in these ways when planning or participating in activities or traditions?

  What are some ways in which we can better incorporate praise, worship, and thankfulness of God into our lives?

DISCUSSION 6

In What Religion Will We Raise Our Children?

Train children in the right way, and when old, they will not stray (Proverbs 22:6).

When our son Matthew was between one and two years old, we took him on a vacation to a beach house on North Carolina's Outer Banks. In one corner on the top floor of the three-story house, two screened windows flanked each other, one facing a deck and one facing the south wall of the house, with a decorative trunk under each. Because the weather was pleasant, Brian and I threw open both windows and foolishly didn't give them another thought. Not until we heard Matthew's cry did we realize that he had crawled onto one of the trunks and pressed against the window screen, popping the screen out. Thankfully, he had picked the window facing the deck and was now lying on the deck, a bit stunned but fine nonetheless because the screen had cushioned his landing. I fear things would have been much different had he chosen the other, identical-looking window.

We learned so many valuable lessons from this experience, not the least of which was to never leave windows open so wide that Matthew could push his body against the screen! Most importantly, though, we learned that no matter how good we think we are as parents, we can never be good enough. We will always fail to recognize some obstacle, some impediment, to our child's well-being. The only way to fully protect our son is to fully entrust him to the care of the one who is the Father of us all. Otherwise, our care of him will be incomplete. Stormie Omartian reiterates this point in *The Power of a Praying Parent* where she emphasizes that, by entrusting our children to God, we don't give up responsibility for them; we establish ourselves in a working partnership with God, where we care for our children within God's "wisdom, power, protection, and ability far beyond ourselves."[88]

As parents, you need to use this same principle in raising your children, fully relying on God to guide them in body, mind, and spirit and guard them from dangers seen and unseen. One of the many ways that God will help you raise your children is to guide you in making the best decisions regarding their religious education and upbringing. Just as God prompted Matthew to choose the best window to explore, God will guide you in making the best decisions for your children—and also for your relationship and every other aspect of your lives. All you have to do is ask for his guidance: "In all your ways acknowledge him, and he will make straight your paths" (Proverbs 3:6). And remember to trust in the guidance for which you ask, and God will enable you to make difficult decisions with peace in your hearts: "Those of steadfast mind you keep in peace—in peace because they trust in you" (Isaiah 26:3).

Because of your role as parents, you have the first and primary responsibility for educating your children. You will begin to teach your children the instant you hold them after they are born. Through your nurturing of them and of each other, you will teach them about the greatest and most important commandment: love. Parents' love for their children reflects God's love for his Son and for all of us as his adopted children. Parents also reflect God to their children by being imitators of Christ, by teaching through the examples of their own righteous lives. And in Psalm 37:25–26, David describes the fruits in children of righteous parents: "I have been young, and now am old, yet I have not seen the righteous forsaken or their children begging bread. They

---

[88]Stormie Omartian, *The Power of a Praying Parent* (Eugene, Ore.: Harvest House Publishers, 1995), 16.

are ever giving liberally and lending, and their children become a blessing."

The religious education of your children is essentially part of the Great Commission that Jesus gave to his disciples: " 'Go therefore and make disciples of all nations, baptizing them in the name of the Father and of the Son and of the Holy Spirit, and teaching them to obey everything that I have commanded you' " (Matthew 28:19–20). Just as you have been instructed in the Christian faith, you have the obligation to pass the faith on to your children, making them disciples of Christ as well. The Bible also reminds us to be sure we fully know, understand, accept, and practice the faith. Otherwise, we won't be able to effectively teach our children: "Walk about Zion, go all around it, count its towers, consider well its ramparts; go through its citadels, that you may tell the next generation that this is God, our God forever and ever" (Psalm 48:12–14).

While you are teaching your children Christian principles by example, you should also begin to explain to them the religious principles of the Christian faith, even before you think they can truly understand. Instruction should be a little at a time, beginning when your children are young, as described in Isaiah 28:10: " 'For it is precept upon precept, precept upon precept, line upon line, line upon line, here a little, there a little.' " Start with simple ideas, "milk," and build upon them, much as Paul did in his teaching of the Corinthian Christians: "I fed you with milk, not solid food, for you were not ready for solid food" (1 Corinthians 3:2).

With Matthew, we started teaching him the basics of the Christian faith as an infant through a Bible made specifically for infants, with very simple, four-line Bible stories. As he matured, we upgraded our Bible to more detailed versions. I also started homeschooling him in what could be considered a pre-preschool when he was about two, where each session was based on a Bible story and principle. I also helped him apply these Bible stories and principles to situations in his young life. One time, he had a bad experience swimming by himself during a swimming lesson, in which the float he was using slipped, and he felt like he was sinking. For weeks after that, he would cling to me in the pool, refusing to swim by himself. We talked about his fear using the example of Peter walking on the water with Jesus (Matthew 14:28–31). Even though Peter was scared, Jesus helped him so that he wouldn't sink, just as he will help you not sink, I told Matthew. Eventually, Matthew regained his confidence and was able to swim independently again. When educating your children, look for opportunities like this to use Bible stories and principles in everyday applications.

As parents united in an interfaith relationship, you have several aspects to consider regarding how you will religiously educate your children. You want to raise them in the Christian faith, yet don't want to bias them toward the Catholic or Protestant practice of the faith because both faith traditions are important to you. On the other hand, you do want your children to know about and appreciate the religious backgrounds in which both of you were raised. Then you have the added challenge of integrating all these elements within the guidelines for raising children set forth by the Catholic Church and perhaps even by your specific Protestant church or denomination.

First, you must decide in what denomination to raise your children, what church you will attend as a family. Specific suggestions for choosing a church are provided in *Discussion 4: What Church Will We Attend After We Marry?*, which starts on page 217. You should decide how you will publicly practice your faith as a family *before* you even have children. By choosing a church or churches early in your relationship, you not only establish yourself in a routine but you also help simplify the making of necessary decisions in your child's young life, such as when and where and even if to have your child baptized or dedicated as an infant.

In addition to choosing a church for your family, you must choose how you want to formally religiously educate your children. It is a good idea to also think these options through before you have children to avoid having to make hasty, time-critical decisions that could cause conflicts within your family. Here are some options available to you for incorporating religion into your children's education at various stages of their lives:

- Pre-preschool—informal, home-based Christian program, for ages 0–3.
- Preschool—Protestant Christian, Catholic (parochial), or homeschool, for ages 3–5.
- Kindergarten/grade school—Protestant Christian, Catholic (parochial), or homeschool, for ages 5–12.
- Confraternity of Christian Doctrine (CCD) classes— Catholic, offered on Saturdays, Sundays, or evenings during the week, for ages 5–18.
- Sunday school—Protestant and Catholic, offered on Sundays, usually for preschool through adult ages.
- Junior high school/high school—Protestant Christian, Catholic (parochial), or homeschool, for ages 12–18.
- College—Protestant Christian, Catholic, for ages 18+

Secular options are also available for preschool through college, which could be combined with other forms of religious education. Also be sure to check the educational classes offered by your area zoos, museums, symphonies, science centers, art galleries, parks, and nature reserves. And your church may have Bible studies, music ministries, missionary opportunities, and other activities with which your children can become involved.

Because you each have a rich religious heritage and background, you should be creative in integrating aspects of your faith traditions into your children's education. For example, you may choose to attend a Protestant church and enroll your children in the church's Sunday school program while the children attend a public school and CCD classes during the week. Or you may want to attend a Catholic church but have your children attend a Protestant Christian school and CCD classes in the evening. In our family, we attend the Catholic Church primarily and the Protestant church occasionally, and Matthew attends a nondenominational Protestant Christian school and Sunday school at the Protestant church. When he is older, he will most likely attend a public school and CCD classes in order to receive instruction for the sacraments.

When making decisions about raising your children, it is important to keep in mind the Catholic Church's requirements regarding the religious upbringing of children in an interfaith marriage. Before marriage, the Catholic partner is asked to do his or her best to see that any children are baptized Catholic and raised in the Catholic Church, based upon the Catholic Church's belief that its teachings and priests have roots in the original apostolic church. The Catholic Church doesn't make the Catholic "promise" to do so because it does take into account the non-Catholic parent's rights and responsibilities in raising the children as well. In the past, the non-Catholic partner was required to promise to raise the children Catholic, but no such promise or commitment is required today.

Some parents in an interfaith relationship don't want to make religious decisions for their children, so they decide to wait until each child is old enough to personally choose a religion. In one interfaith family we know, some of the children attend a Catholic church, while the others attend a Protestant church, at the direction of their parents. I have even heard the ridiculous suggestion that a family refrain from choosing a family church until the first child is born, letting the child's sex determine what church to attend! For obvious reasons, none of these options is the best for you or your children. Thomas and Thomas note, "Children are always learning, whether you intend it or not. In this case, they are learning that religion is not important to either of their parents."[89]

Not making religious decisions also lets your children see that there are religious divisions between you, weakening the spiritual basis of your family. You should, however, acknowledge that you may have differences in non-core beliefs and explain the source of those differences. Your purpose shouldn't be to have your children choose one religion over the other or to think that one way of practicing the faith is better than the other. You should simply want your children to understand the faith backgrounds from which you, their parents, came. Most

---

[89]Thomas, *Beginning Your Marriage*, 189.

importantly, emphasize to your children all of the Christian beliefs that you have discovered you hold in common. Just as these common core beliefs have strengthened your interfaith relationship, they can strengthen your familial bonds with your children as well.

No matter what educational options you choose for your children, another responsibility you have for them as their parents is to pray for them throughout their lives: "Pour out your heart like water before the presence of the Lord! Lift your hands to him for the lives of your children" (Lamentations 2:19). Pray for your children's health, well-being, protection, education, talents, spirituality, and any other concerns that may arise throughout their lives.

Relationship Builders

- As parents, you need to fully entrust your children to the care of God.
  Have we been guilty as parents of relying on ourselves as sole guardians of our children?
  What problems with our children could have been helped or prevented through a deeper reliance on God?

- Parents are the primary educators of their children.
  Have we made conscious efforts to teach our children about the Christian faith?
  Have we presented the doctrines of both of our religions to our children?

- Identify and evaluate all of the available options for religiously educating your children.
  What educational options are offered by our church or local Christian and parochial schools?
  What are some ways in which we can creatively combine options to give our children a well-rounded education?

- Your children need your prayers.
  Do we pray for our children?
  On what aspects of our children's lives should we focus our prayers?

DISCUSSION 7

How Do We Respond to Questions, Comments, and Pressures from our Families and Friends?

Honor your father and your mother, so that your days may be long in the land that the LORD your God is giving you (Exodus 20:12).

When you decide to commit to each other in marriage, you not only marry that person but essentially marry his or her entire family, many other people who have influenced that person throughout his or her life. And that could be good or bad, particularly regarding your interfaith issues. You have chosen to work through this book most likely because you have disagreements with either the Catholic or Protestant religion of your partner. Your attitude toward your partner's religion has probably developed based upon what you were taught from your parents and other family members and friends.

Discussion 7

In my family, most everyone is Catholic, so I was raised that the Catholic religion was the right one to follow. Protestants weren't condemned to hell because of their beliefs; they just weren't following the whole truth.

"I was raised Protestant, although my dad was once Catholic, and a large part of his family is still Catholic," says Brian. "At some points, I was taught to be wary of the dubious nature of Catholic practices. Some of my friends have even gone so far as to say that practicing Catholics are not true Christians."

Has either of you had a similar experience, where you feel your prejudices toward Catholicism or Protestantism are based on the influences of your family and close friends? If so, even though you may have worked through your differences yourselves, your families and friends still most likely hold on to the beliefs they always have. And this could create problems for your interfaith relationship.

The Bible tells us that we must honor our father and mother, first stated in the commandment God gave to Moses (Exodus 20:12) and then reiterated by Paul in Ephesians 6:2–3. But Jesus also states in Matthew 10:37, " 'Whoever loves father or mother more than me is not worthy of me.' " What Jesus is saying here is that you need to put him first in your lives and in your relationship. If you sincerely believe that God is calling you to be with this person, in spite of anything your families or friends say about his or her religious beliefs, you must put your relationship, established and blessed by God, first. Doing so is not dishonoring your parents; contrarily, it is honoring God. (Obviously, by this I am referring to two Christians in a relationship. However, God may have reasons for calling a Christian and a non-Christian together, although one must be very cautious in this type of relationship. See *Discussion 2: Are We Unequally Yoked?* on page 205 for more about this kind of spiritually unbalanced relationship.)

Even if your relationship goes against what your parents and other family members or friends may want, you must continue to treat them with the respect they deserve as Christians who are only conveying what they genuinely believe to be true. Your parents may be concerned that you are abandoning the religion and faith beliefs that they worked so hard to instill and may even fear that you or your children will not be saved. Your parents may also feel guilty or inadequate. In addition, they may be concerned that you are giving up the faith you will need when tough times come.

You need to address the concerns of your families and friends clothed with the fruits of the Holy Spirit: love, joy, peace, patience, charity, goodness, chastity, modesty, kindness, generosity, faithfulness, gentleness, and self-control. Gently explain to them that you understand their concerns, and reassure them that neither you nor your partner has abandoned God and the Christian faith and are still saved. Acknowledge that what you are anchoring your relationship on are the core Christian beliefs that you have discovered you hold in common, despite any denominational differences. You could also explain how this relationship has not made you move away from God but rather grow deeper in your faith, and perhaps even share with your families some of the insights that you and your partner have received through prayer and discussion. And perhaps through your varied discussions with your partner, you have grown even more appreciative of and committed to your original religion. You could share those insights with your families and friends as well.

You may find it difficult or uncomfortable to talk with your families about these interfaith issues. If this is the case, remember the words that Jesus spoke to the twelve apostles: " '[D]o not worry about how you are to speak or what you are to say; for what you are to say will be given to you at that time; for it is not you who speak, but the Spirit of your Father speaking through you' " (Matthew 10:19–20). Pray for the intercession of the Holy Spirit, and you will know exactly what to say to your families and how to say it best.

Although they may not wholly agree with your decisions, keep in mind that your parents are indispensable sources of wisdom for guidance, even in your interfaith relationship. Proverbs says, "Listen to your father who begot you, and do not despise your mother when she is old" (Proverbs 23:22) and "Without counsel, plans go wrong, but with many advisers they succeed" (Proverbs 15:22). Brian's dad was raised Catholic and had at once even considered becoming a Catholic priest. Therefore, he was able to provide Brian with advice and insight that was beneficial to our relationship. Don't be afraid to ask your families for their insights but also remember to sort through all of the advice in prayer, asking for insight into God's will for your life and relationship.

Whatever decisions you have made as a couple, reassure your parents and other concerned family members and friends that you have both prayed about the decisions and truly believe that this is the direction in which God is leading you. But understand that you may not be able to receive complete approval from one or both of your families regarding the decisions you make or even regarding your relationship itself. There may come a time when you need to step out together on your own in Christ, doing what you believe you are called to do as a Christian couple in spite of any familial oppositions. Even in these circumstances, though, don't forget to continually pray for your families and friends, that God will grant them "the spirit of wisdom and under-standing" (Isaiah 11:2) so that, through the intercession of the Holy Spirit, they may understand and perhaps even accept your commitment to each other and to God as united Christians of different denomina-tions.

In all your efforts, go to great lengths to not alienate your families and friends. As much as you think you might not need them now, you will inevitably need them later, for support during the hard times and to celebrate with you during the good times. Each of your families has helped to mold you and make you what you have become and has heavily contributed to the person with which your partner has fallen in love. Just as you have strived to build a unified Christian relationship between yourselves, make an effort to extend that unity outward to envelope your families and friends. The efforts you make now will pay incredible dividends later in the ongoing love and support they can provide to both you and your children.

Relationship Builders

• Families and friends have probably contributed to your denominational prejudices.
  Growing up, what have we been taught about religion?
  In what ways has what we've been taught in the past impacted our interfaith relationship today?
  Are we committed to working through any prejudices that we might hold?

• Families and friends, even though they may disapprove of your interfaith relationship, deserve respect.
  What are the objections raised by our families and friends concerning our relationship?
  How do we feel about these objections?
  Can we understand the sources of the objections and respect our families and friends for saying only what they genuinely believe to be correct?

• The Holy Spirit can be the Helper who guides you in explaining your relationship and religious issues to your families and friends.
  Have we deliberately asked the Holy Spirit for help in talking to our families and friends?
  Do we fully trust in his guidance?

• Sometimes, you may have to do what you know is right for your relationship, even if it means opposing the wishes of your families and friends.
  Is the situation with our families and friends such that we may have to go against what they believe is right?
  Is our love for each other and for God strong enough to take this brave step together in faith?